Teaching Men of Color in the Community College

A Guidebook

CORA

Center for Organizational Responsibility and Advancement

Published by Montezuma Publishing
Please direct comments regarding this product to:

Montezuma Publishing
Aztec Shops Ltd.
San Diego State University
San Diego, California 92182-1701
619-594-7552
or email: orders@montezumapublishing.com
website: www.montezumapublishing.com

Production Credits
Production mastering by: Gianna Punzalan
Quality control by: Scott Leyland

ISBN-10: 0-7442-2952-9
ISBN-13: 978-0-7442-2952-3

TABLE OF CONTENTS

DEDICATION

This book is dedicated to the educators who work with and advocate for men of color.

ACKNOWLEDGEMENTS

The authors of this guidebook would like to acknowledge faculty members who contributed to this study. Some of these faculty members included: Hector S. Menchaca, Tarrant County College-Trinity River Campus; Maurice Johnson, Community College of Baltimore County; Larry McGhee Sr., Triton College; Thekima Mayasa, San Diego Mesa College; Larry Burns, MiraCosta College; Lawrence E. Norris, Lone Star College-CyFair; Tony R. Fitch, San Joaquin Delta College; Kyle Owens, Cal State San Marcos; Sheldon Lewis Smart, Tarrant County College, Trinity River Campus; Misael C. Camarena, San Diego City College; Vernon Jones, Broward College; Marques Washington, Eastfield College; Elva Salinas, San Diego City College; Sylvia Aguirre-Alberto, College of San Mateo; Krystal Danielle Romero, College of San Mateo; Anthony Merritt, Mesa College; and Rudy Ramirez, College of San Mateo.

The authors would also like to recognize the Minority Male Community College Collaborative (M2C3) project team, including: Soua Xiong, Angelica Palacios, Arthur Tovar, Jamal Mazyck, James Bolden, Vannessa Falcon, Tom del la Garza, Tyler Davis, as well as Dr. Marissa Vasquez Urias.

PREFACE

Advancing the success of men of color in the community college has been a topic of intensified concern among educators in recent years. Much of the interest has focused on Black and Latino men, though challenges facing Southeast Asian (SEA), Pacific Islander (PI), and Native American men are becoming increasingly recognized (Harris & Wood, 2014b; Wood, Harris & Xiong, 2014). Challenges facing these men in community college are evidenced by outcome gaps between them and their White and Asian (non-SEA/PI) peers. Outcomes data for Black and Latino men help to demonstrate this point. In community colleges, only 32.1% and 30.2% of Black and Latino men, respectively will earn a certificate, degree, or transfer to a four-year college within a six-year time frame. In contrast, 39.8% of White and 43.4% of Asian (non-SEA/PI) men will do so in the period. Possibly more concerning than these gaps are the deleterious success rates of Black and Latino men who attend community colleges part-time. Approximately 15% of Black and 25% of Latino men attend community colleges exclusively part-time (though many others have mixed part-time and full-time enrollment). For these exclusive part-timers, only 4.3% of Black and 7.4% of Latino men will attain their goals within a six-year time frame (BPS, 2009).

In response to these data, there has been a proliferation of initiatives, conferences, summits, and programs focused on addressing the capacity of community colleges to retain, graduate, and transfer men of color (Harris & Wood, 2014b). In fact, so many efforts have been undertaken, that the American Association of Community Colleges (AACC) created a national database to catalogue these efforts and their programmatic functions (Christian, 2010). While the structure of initiatives designed to improve outcomes for men of color in community colleges varies greatly, the core commitment has been to redress disparities that systematically disadvantage these men. In wider society, the concern for the educational realities and life outcomes of males of color has been echoed by the Obama administration. In February of 2014, the administration launched the My Brother's Keeper (MBK) initiative. Bolstered by funding from private foundations and organizations, the goal of MBK was to create enhanced opportunities for boys and young men of color to succeed in society (The Seven Centers, 2014).

In recognizing the linkage between success in education and outcomes in health, criminal justice systems, and social services, MBK has overwhelmingly focused on education as *the* critical site for intervention (Harper & Wood, 2015). With respect to postsecondary education, MBK espouses that "every American child should have the option to attend postsecondary education and receive the education and training needed for quality jobs of today and tomorrow" (White House, 2014, para 3). Community colleges have and continue to serve as the primary pathway into postsecondary education for men of color (Bush & Bush, 2010). In fact, 71% of Black and Latino men begin their experiences in public postsecondary education at community colleges. They do so, with the belief that these institutions will foster their upward social and economic mobility so they can compete for the 'jobs of today and tomorrow'.

Given the sheer number of men of color in community colleges, the institution's commitment to open access education and local community needs, these colleges are uniquely situated to create new life opportunities for men of color, their families, and their communities. However, doing so will require critical capacity building among community college professionals, particularly those who have the most opportunities to support men of color (e.g., faculty, counselors, advisors). Faculty members are among those college professionals most readily positioned to support the success of men of color. They have the most structured opportunities to interact with these men, particularly in the classroom. Bearing this in mind, this guidebook serves as a framework to empower faculty to support the teaching and learning enterprise of men of color. This is accomplished by addressing common barriers faced by these men, promising practices for teaching and learning, and recommendations for instructional leadership.

The timeliness and importance of this guidebook in serving as a resource for faculty in community colleges cannot be understated. In this current era of accountability, improving outcomes for all students (especially those on the 'margins' of academic institutions) is a top priority. The general public and policymakers have become increasingly focused on student success (Nevarez & Wood, 2010). Emblematic of this focus was the initiation of the American Graduation Initiative (AGI) in 2009, which sought to increase the total number of community college certificate and degree earners by five million, by the year 2020. At the state level, policymakers have implemented graduation goals, policy reforms, and statewide collaborations designed to ensure that community colleges (and other postsecondary institutions) support the public interest in developing graduates to meet national labor market needs (Mullin, 2012; Wood & Harrison, 2015).

In this context, men of color represent a key demographic group that can support the nation in filling critical intellectual and leadership needs. Moreover, faculty members are among those most central to supporting community colleges in advancing student success. By implementing classroom practices that benefit students who are on the academic margins of the institution, they will be better positioned to benefit all students, regardless of background. To be clear, the strategies that *work* with educating men of color are in line with strategies that *work* for all students. However, due to societal pressures, external life challenges, and alienating campus climates, men of color reap an intensified benefit from 'good' teaching strategies and approaches.

All Faculty Can Teach Men of Color

To be clear, all faculty members' regardless of their racial/ethnic or gender background *can* effectively teach men of color. We believe that there are four essential elements that can effectively foster academic success for men of color (see Figure 1). In the 1960's, Nevitt Sanford espoused that student success in college was a function of two factors, challenge and support. Sanford (1966) proffered that students must be *challenged* academically with rigorous coursework. As such, lectures, assignments, discussions, and out-of-class work should challenge students to higher academic horizons. Students should be challenged to become higher-order thinkers who can learn, apply, and critique extant theories and models within their respective academic disciplines. However, challenge cannot occur in isolation. Sanford argued that challenge must be accompanied with *support*.

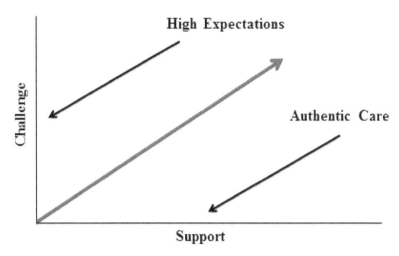

Figure 1. Four elements of faculty excellence for teaching men of color.

The authors conceptualize support as entailing direct support from course instructors in learning the academic content as well as the existence, accessibility, and efficacy of critical campus services (e.g., tutoring, advising, library). Students must be aware of available support, perceive available support as being reliable, and know that it can meet their needs. As noted by Sanford (1966), there is an optimal balance between challenge and support. Too much challenge and too little support can create an environment where students' needs are unattended, resulting in frustration and potential departure. In contrast, when there is little challenge and too much support, students can take learning for granted, become disengaged due to a lack of rigor, and exhibit disinterest in their education. Given this, Sanford suggested that high levels of both challenge and support are necessary conditions for the success of students.

While Sanford's notions of challenge and support are critical components of students' academic and personal growth, the authors of this guidebook believe that two additional components are also needed. For men of color (and other historically underrepresented and underserved students), preconditions must be set prior to both challenge and support to actualize student success. Prior to challenge, high expectations and belief in students' ability to succeed must be foregrounded. Students must know that faculty members believe in their ability to succeed at high levels of performance. *High expectations* must be communicated to students through both verbal and non-verbal actions. Given the socially engrained perceptions of men of color as unintelligent, high expectations are necessary to disrupt prior messages of inferiority and communicate to students that they are believed to be capable. Thus, with high expectations, students will feel empowered to meet academic challenges set forth before them in the classroom.

Challenge and high expectations must also be met with support. That being said, support may be available and efficacious, but if faculty and staff do not communicate an *authentic care* for the student, then the support may go unused. Students must believe that faculty members authentically care about them, personally and academically. Without authenticity, students may be weary of using support services that could provide opportunities to reify potential fears they may have about their academic abilities. Given the apprehension of many men, particularly men of color, to seek out help from faculty and staff when needed (Wood, 2014), authentic care can reduce their apprehension to engage support by fostering a foundation of trust between faculty and students.

When faculty members' challenge and support of students are prefixed with high expectations and authentic care, the necessary conditions for student success are fostered. Regardless of background, faculty members who embody these four elements in their relationships and teaching practice with men of color will experience greater levels of success. Even when mistakes and missteps are made in navigating differences in cultural terrains, faculty employing these four elements of teaching excellence will be empowered to better educate men of color. Next, we describe the process by which the promising practices offered in this brief were identified.

The Process of Identifying Promising Practices

The content presented in this guidebook is derived from five primary sources of information. First, the authors conducted an extensive review of extant research on men of color in community colleges with a focus on scholarly publications (e.g., peer-reviewed journal articles, book chapters, reports) that addressed teaching and learning, student development, campus climates, and faculty-student engagement. Second, the researchers conducted interviews with men of color in community colleges. A total of 35 men of color were interviewed to determine factors that influenced their success in community college, from their perspectives. Several recurrent themes emanating from these interviews highlighted the role that faculty have in building healthy conditions for classroom engagement.

Third, the researchers collected 'narratives of success' from men of color who had transferred from a community college to a four-year institution. Most of the narratives were from men of color who had recently (within the past few years) earned a baccalaureate degree and were enrolled in graduate programs in counseling, college student affairs, and postsecondary education. These narratives addressed successful relationships with faculty at both the sending and receiving institutions. Fourth, the researchers also employed quantitative data from the Community College Survey of Men (CCSM). The CCSM is an institutional-level needs assessment tool that has been used by over 40 community colleges in eight states (e.g., Arizona, Arkansas, California, Illinois, Maryland, Minnesota, Pennsylvania, Texas) to examine factors that influence male student success (de la Garza, Wood & Harris, 2014; Wood & Harris, 2013). With respect to the focus of this guidebook, a significant portion of the CCSM is dedicated to campus ethos factors (e.g., climate, culture) that assess faculty members' relationships with men of color.

Finally, to identify promising practices relevant to teaching and learning for men of color in community colleges, insights from faculty members who have been successful in serving Black, Latino, Native American, and Southeast Asian men were sought. These faculty members are referred to as 'faculty leaders' throughout this guidebook. Specifically, authors communicated with community college leaders to identify faculty members who had success in serving men from historically underrepresented and underserved groups. These leaders were asked to identify two faculty members who could contribute strategies to this guidebook. To contribute to the promising practices identified herein, faculty members had to satisfy three criterion. They must have: (a) been a faculty member for at least four years; (b) had a "track record" of successfully serving men of color; and (c) illustrated success in serving men of color both in-and out-of the classroom. In all, 27 faculty members contributed to this guidebook. Of these contributors, 96% agreed that the teaching and learning experience of men of color requires enhanced strategies. Specifically, these contributors pointed to the role of external life stressors (e.g., familial obligations, financial responsibilities, transportation concerns) and male of color socialization as being primary motives for enhanced teaching strategies.

Guidebook Outline

This guidebook is divided into four main parts. In *Part 1: Foundations of Success for Men of Color,* the theoretical perspectives undergirding a revised teaching and learning enterprise that prioritizes the success of men of color are discussed. Also explored are common barriers and challenges facing men of color that necessitate enhanced teaching practices. A key focus of these barriers are on environmental factors (external pressures that occur outside of college that influence student success in college) and on the socialization of men of color in education. Parts II and III articulate the promising practices derived from the comprehensive study of faculty. Specifically, *Part II: Building Relationships with Men of Color* discusses the establishment of personal relationships with men of color as a foundational precursor to efficacious teaching practices. In *Part III: Promising Teaching Practices*, the authors address the role of relevancy and interactivity (among other factors) in effectively communicating academic content to men of color. The guidebook concludes with *Part IV: A Note to Instructional Leaders* with strategies that academic leaders can employ to inculcate the values and approaches discussed in this volume in their departments and colleges.

PART I

FOUNDATIONS OF SUCCESS FOR MEN OF COLOR

The purpose of this chapter is to provide the contextual foundation necessary to engage the teaching and learning content presented in this guidebook. In laying this foundation, three primary areas of focus are addressed: (1) factors necessitating enhanced teaching and learning strategies; (2) the institutional responsibility perspective on student success; and (3) the Socio-Ecological Outcomes (SEO) model that guided the conceptualization of factors influencing outcomes for men of color in community colleges. Faculty leaders were asked to identify factors impeding the success of men of color in community college classrooms. Faculty provided numerous personal and institutional challenges that affect student success. Collectively, challenges and social pressures demonstrate that the enhanced teaching and learning strategies identified in this guidebook are necessary. Four interrelated areas necessitating enhanced strategies are discussed below, they include: external pressures, racial-gender stereotypes, male gender role socialization, and under-preparedness for collegiate work.

Factors Necessitating Enhanced
Teaching and Learning Strategies

External Pressures

Faculty leaders identified the role of environmental pressures (factors that occur outside of college that influence students' lives inside of college) as important considerations in student success for men of color. Specifically, faculty noted that *some* men of color lack financial resources, which can inhibit their access to necessary course materials and reliable transportation. Indeed, a large percentage of men of color in the community college are of low income backgrounds. Using the federal TRIO definition (of an household income of $25,000 or less), the majority of Black, Native American, and Hispanic/Latino men are classified as low income, at 59%, 59%, and 48%, respectively. In contrast, 33% of White men are considered low income (NPSAS, 2012). Commuting to and from college can be a barrier for many low-income students who may need to rely upon public transportation services to attend college. Commuting can detract from the time students would otherwise place on academically related matters (e.g., meeting with faculty, participating in campus study groups, using essential campus services). Regardless of the mode of transportation (e.g., bus, car, train), data derived from the CCSM indicated that 50% of Black men, 45% of Mexican American men, and 48% of Latino (non-Mexicano) men, report spending at least six hours or more commuting to and from campus. In comparison, only 33% of White men indicated doing so.

Pressures facing low-income men can be further heightened when they are responsible for supporting the financial needs of others (e.g., children, partners, parents, grandparents). Faculty leaders noted that many men of color have external commitments to work and family that can pull their time away from focusing on academic matters. For instance, Black and Native American men are significantly more likely than their peers to have financial dependents (NPSAS, 2012). Given social pressures for men to serve as breadwinners, having dependents can require men to focus their time on providing for others rather than developing themselves academically. As such, it should not be surprising that across racial/ethnic groups, men who are employed work 32-33 hours per week. However, research on men of color (particularly Black men) demonstrates that these men are concentrated in jobs that are physically demanding (e.g., moving boxes, stocking shelves), have late night shifts, and face employment options that are often temporary or transitional in nature (Wood, 2010). Thus, the very nature of the work available to these men can make success in school more difficult.

Additional external pressures faced by some men of color are stressful life events. Stressful life events encompass a wide range of challenging circumstances and experiences that can serve to detract students' focus/effort from school. Examples of stressful life events include: divorce, loss of job(s), eviction, relationship breakup, incarceration, major change at work, illness in the family, and death of a close friend or family member. All community college men experience high numbers of stressful life events. Data from the CCSM indicate that, on average, men across racial/ethnic groups encountered four or more stressful life events in the past two years. For some men, the total number of events can be even more acute. For example, 15% of Latino men experienced seven or more stressful life events in the past two years. Taken together, the environmental pressures facing men of color (e.g., finances, familial obligations, work commitments, life stress) can detract from the time and resources necessary to properly engage in college.

Racial-Gender Stereotypes

It may be difficult for some faculty members to accept the fact that racism and stereotypes still permeate American society. While typically subtle and unconsciously communicated, stereotypes can shape the lived realities of men of color inside and outside of the classroom. As a result, faculty leaders overwhelmingly discussed the social perceptions and stereotypes of men of color. This guidebook was written in the wake of the shooting death of Michael Brown, one among many high profile killings involving men of color (e.g., Trayvon Martin, Eric Garner, Oscar Grant III, Amadou Diallo) in recent years. Unfortunately, these events demonstrate that boys and men of color continue to be perceived and engaged as criminals by wider society. The perception of young men of color as indolent, criminal deviants is evident. Data derived from the CCSM demonstrate that noticeable percentages of men of color believe that professors hold negative stereotypes about men from their racial/ethnic and gender groups. In fact, 23% of Southeast Asian and 21% of Black men believe so.

While perception may not always be reality, it is important to recognize that some men of color may experience college in ways that are marginalizing and alienating, which they attribute to their race/ethnicity. Thus, their perceptions of stereotypes are valid and should be readily acknowledged. Schools and colleges, as a microcosm of wider society, reflect the criminalized view of boys and men of color. This view has direct implications for how males of color are treated and engaged by a K-12 teacher and postsecondary faculty member that is not racially reflective of them. Unfortunately, while some faculty members may see a Black or Latino male student with incredible talent, others may see a 'menace to society.' Some faculty members may not be as welcoming to men of color or invite interactions with them inside and outside of class (e.g., on campus, during office hours) for fear of them.

The racialized experiences of men of color originate from early years of schooling. Long before college, boys of color learn that they are perceived as deviants and are responded to rashly. For years, K-12 scholars have documented how boys of color have been systematically tracked into special education programs for "behavioral" issues that reflect a deeply engrained 'fear' for these males. In many instances, special education has become a concentrated area for boys of color rather than a site to support children who need supplemental support. The disproportionately high use of exclusionary discipline practices with boys of color is also indicative of this perspective. Young men of color are significantly more likely than their male peers to be suspended and expelled from school, often for actions on par with that of other boys, but perceived very differently by educators (The Seven Centers Report, 2014). By the time students reach college, these experiences can shape their perceptions on the value of school, their trust in faculty members, and their engagement in the classroom. Altogether, real experiences with racism, as well as the influence of negative perceptions of men of color as unintelligent and criminal, can affect the educational realities of these men in college.

Male Gender Socialization

Patterns of male gender role socialization also factor heavily into men of color's schooling experiences. At early ages, boys are taught to express themselves as males by being tough, aggressive, unemotional, and through other behaviors that are socially constructed as masculine. Harris and Harper (2008) discussed several key influences on male gender role socialization and the ways in which it shapes academic outcomes for boys and young men. Among them were parents and families, male peer groups, and schools. Boys who are raised in two-parent homes often observe a gendered division of household labor and duties. For example, mothers often assume responsibility for child rearing, preparing meals, cleaning the home, and other activities that are associated with femininity. Conversely, men often take on the roles of breadwinner, disciplinarian, and other responsibilities that are socially constructed as masculine. Moreover, patterns of male gender role socialization are reflected in the toys that are purchased for boys, the games they are taught to play, and the strategies that are employed for rewarding and punishing behavior. Collectively, these gendered interactions that take place in the home reinforce societal messages about what is assumed to be normative behavior for boys and men, laying a foundation for the ways in which they pursue learning and academic endeavors. We see these messages manifest quite acutely in school settings, particularly an apprehension to openly engage in academic activities, refusal to ask for help, and over-prioritizing sports and other male-dominated activities, to name a few.

Male peer group interactions also weigh heavily on the gender socialization of boys and young men. Male peers often reinforce messages about gender and masculinity that are introduced and practiced in the home. Physicality, overt heterosexism, and a disdain for anything that is associated with femininity are values and behaviors that afford young men status and respect from male peers. Thus, it is not surprising that boys who are athletically gifted and successful in gaining attention from girls are typically the most popular amongst their male peers. Yet boys who are "smart," not good at sports, and not deemed physically attractive, often have their masculinities questioned and branded as "sissys," "nerds," and "squares." These same young men are also the targets of bullying, harassment, and social alienation from male peers, which can have longstanding emotional consequences. Therefore, boys and young men enact strategic efforts to put their "coolness" on display for male peers, and even going so far as to outright reject behaviors and pursuits that position them for academic success.

In school settings, teachers and other educators engage boys and young men of color based on socially constructed notions of masculinity and unintentionally reinforce patterns of gender role socialization. Traditionally, in the classroom, boys are encouraged to engage in masculine oriented activities, such as playing with building blocks, whereas girls are encouraged to engage in dramatic play and other activities that are assumed to be feminine (Alloway, 1995). Gendered interactions that characterize relationships between boys and young men of color and K-12 educators are perhaps most evident in disciplinary practices by which these students are suspended and expelled at rates that far exceed their White and female peers. These issues are further complicated by the overrepresentation of White female teachers who may enter schooling contexts from a cultural standpoint that is not aligned with that of their male students of color. Moreover, the underrepresentation of men of color as classroom teachers lead some boys of color to reason that school is not a domain that is suited for them and their long term life success.

One notable deleterious effect of the aforementioned patterns of male gender role socialization is an irrational fear of femininity and anxiety about being perceived as unmanly among men. Psychologist James O'Neil (1981) conceptualized this phenomenon as "male gender role conflict" (MGRC) and identified six behavioral patterns that manifest acutely among men as a result of it. Among these patterns are a difficulty expressing emotions and vulnerability (restricted emotionality), a need to assume power and control over others (socialized power, control, and competition), and homophobia, to name some. O'Neil and his colleagues found that males often enact destructive and unhealthy strategies to relieve tension and anxiety that results from discrepancies between their authentic selves and socially constructed ideologies of what a man *should* be. Far too often, for men of color this entails devaluing academic learning and success.

Lack of Preparation for Collegiate Work

Faculty leaders also noted that *some* men of color may lack the appropriate preparation for collegiate-level coursework. They stated that academic content, as well as time management, study skills, and other necessary academic abilities, may be insufficiently developed. It is accurate to note that men of color are more likely than their White male counterparts to have lower levels of preparation for community college. For example, in 2012, while only 33% of White men required remedial coursework, 44% of Black and Latino men took remedial courses. That being said, the overall developmental needs of all community college students are high. In fact, 41% of all community college students have taken at least one remedial course. To be clear, this does not represent a statistically higher remedial rate for men of color in comparison to the general population (NPSAS, 2012).

Men of color are more likely than other students to have remedial needs across multiple subject areas (e.g., reading, writing, mathematics). For instance, while 15.3%, 18.5%, and 13.2% of Black, Native American, and Latino men require remediation in multiple subject areas; only 8% of White men do. They may also be more likely to need deeper levels of remediation, requiring two or more courses in given content areas (e.g., math, reading, writing). Thus, the remedial needs of these men may be more acute. Notwithstanding, developmental needs should also be considered in context of the schools in which the majority of boys of color are educated. A recent report released by seven research centers that focus explicitly on issues facing boys and men of color in education helps to contextualize challenges facing collegiate preparation:

> Students of color are disproportionately concentrated in schools with underqualified and less experienced educators. In contrast, certified teachers with greater levels of experience are more likely to teach in

predominantly White and affluent schools. The limited numbers of qualified teachers who do teach in majority-minority schools are retained at lower rates, and often transition to schools with greater resources that can provide enhanced job security. Given these dynamics, the least capable teachers too often teach students that demand the most qualified teachers. (The Seven Centers Report, 2014, p. 8)

Limited preparation for collegiate work should not be interpreted as an inability to succeed in college or a lack of desire to do so. The mere presence of men of color in college, despite the numerous social messages they receive throughout their lives communicating that school is not for them, is indicative of their desire to succeed.

The confluence of the aforementioned areas of concern can intensify the challenges faced by men of color. High levels of external life pressures, experiences with racism and pervasive stereotypes, and inadequate preparation for college can erroneously extend stereotypes about cognitive ability. In particular, these challenges can work collectively to reduce necessary dispositions about students' perceived ability to succeed (self-efficacy), the usefulness of college (degree utility), and feelings of control over their academic futures (locus of control). Thus, the multifarious effects of diverse challenges should be acknowledged by faculty members. However, as will be explicated in the next section, these challenges do not remove the responsibility of the institution to support student success but rather, heighten the importance of concerted efforts that advance success for men of color.

Institutional Responsibility:
A Necessary Disposition for Change

Across the country, college educators have expressed a sense of urgency to 'fix' the problems facing men of color. Much of college programming directed towards men of color has focused on building students' capacity to be more self-determined, engaged, and focused in school (Harper, 2014). However, rarely addressed are the structural barriers that create disparate outcomes for men of color. From the perspectives of the guidebook authors, enhanced strategies are necessary for producing conditions on college campuses that support male of color success. W. Edward Deming is attributed as stating that, "every system is perfectly designed to achieve the results it gets." Thus, in order to advance student success for men of color, systemic changes may be necessary. Much of this change begins with (re)specifying the perspectives of college professionals.

The vast majority of educators have been trained to view poor student performance as a function of the students, their families, and their communities. This perspective emanates from foundational student success theories and models which position the student (and their attributes) as the locus of causality for student success. Thus, from this viewpoint, when a student is not successful, the *reason* for failure is the student (Wood & Palmer, 2014). Estela Bensimon (2005) addressed this perspective in her articulation of cognitive frames. She noted that cognitive frames are interpretive frameworks by which college professionals make meaning of student outcomes. She noted that when students are blamed for inadequate outcomes, that this is evidence of a deficit cognitive frame. Bensimon noted that the deficit frame is rooted in

12

stereotypical perceptions of social class, racial/ethnic affiliation, and the 'culture of disadvantage.' She stated that practitioners who are guided by this frame envision educational programming as efforts to remediate or 'fix' the students that they serve. This frame is ubiquitous in postsecondary education, and is embodied within the foundational theories on student success. Scholars from this orientation suggest that student success is based on:

- **Quality of Student Effort** - "If students expect to benefit from what this college or university has to offer, they have to take the initiative…[and are] accountable for the amount, scope and quality of effort they invest in their own learning" (Pace, 1984, pp. 1-2),
- **Academic and Social Integration** - "the problems associated with separation and transition to college are conditions that, though stressful, need not in themselves lead to departure. It is the *individual's response* to those conditions that finally determines staying or leaving" (Tinto, 1987, p. 98),
- **Time on Task** - "the amount of time that *the student* is actively involved in learning" (Anderson, 1975, p. 1),
- **Student Engagement** – "the more *students study* a subject, the more *they know* about it, and the more *students practice* and get feedback from faculty and staff members on *their writing* and collaborative problem solving, the deeper *they come* to understand what *they are* learning" (Kuh, 2009, p. 5), and
- **Student Involvement** - "the amount of physical and psychological energy that *the student* devotes to the academic experiences" (Astin, 1984, p. 298).

(italics added throughout for emphasis)

These theories, while certainly insightful, fail to acknowledge the power within educators to enhance outcomes for students in college. Ascribing to these theories as an explanation for poor student outcomes may be easier for some educators in reconciling inequities, especially when considering the intense external pressures (e.g., familial obligations, work commitments) facing these men. However, as noted by Harris, Bensimon and Bishop (2010), "it is futile to dwell on students' past experiences. It is also harmful if inequalities are rationalized as beyond the control of practitioners. [Instead] we must focus on what *is* within the control of educators in terms of changing their own practices to meet the needs and circumstances of men of color" (p. 280).

Another commonly employed cognitive frame utilized by postsecondary practitioners is the diversity frame. The diversity frame shifts the focus on student success away from deficit notions to focus more clearly on the importance of representational diversity (Bensimon, 2005). Specifically, through this lens, diversity is interpreted as being a legitimate and compelling interest solely through the role of providing opportunities for majority students to be exposed to diverse students. The perceived benefit of this compositional diversity is often associated with the enhanced preparation of majority students to engage in a global marketplace as a result of culturally diverse student-to-student interactions (Bensimon, 2005). In this lens, advocacy for students of color is a result of what *they* can provide to the collegiate environment. As a result, when the diversity frame is employed, a lack of focus on institutional responsibility and student outcomes is evident.

Training and standards geared towards improving male of color success in college should be re-oriented through a lens that focuses on the role of 'campus effort' and 'campus ethos' in student success (Bensimon, 2005). This perspective is espoused by Bensimon (2005) as the equity cognitive frame. The equity frame demonstrates a commitment to institutional practice and outcomes that foster success for historically underrepresented and underserved students. This frame employs a critical viewpoint that seeks to identify disparities and the institutional structures that produce them. The equity frame is focused on remediating institutional personnel (e.g., faculty, staff, administration), as opposed to the students that they serve. As a result, institutional responsibility is the key focus of the equity frame. This includes "institutional responsibility for student outcomes, the manifestation of institutionalized racism, color-conscious[ness], awareness of racialized practices and their differential consequences, [and] awareness of white privilege" (p. 103).

Guided by the equity cognitive frame, Wood and Palmer (2014) extended the Context, Actions, and Outcomes (C-A-O) model as a framework for addressing student success for men of color in college. The C-A-O model counters Astin's (1993) I-E-O model, which views student success as a function of student 'input' characteristics (I), their involvement in the academic and social 'environment' in college (E), and their academic 'outcomes' (O). In contrast, Wood and Palmer noted that a healthier perspective on student success focuses on the institutional 'context' (C) (e.g., institutional history, revenue streams, location, institutional size) to provide an understanding of institutions' capacity to serve men of color. The crux of their model includes the 'actions' (A) that an institution employs and aligns to better serve men of color. They articulate eight primary domains of institutional responsibility for male of color success in college, including:

1. campus resources – necessary for building capacity and sustaining student success efforts;
2. campus climates – that are organized around the values of critical agency, affirmation, and anti-racist dialogue;
3. institutional practices – that feature intrusive, strategic, and collaborative efforts to improve student success that are guided by culturally relevant services and pedagogy;
4. campus structures – that promote access, a sense of belonging, and seek to ensure proportionality among college personnel by relevant demographic characteristics;
5. programs – that focus on high impact practices for engagement and build student's' socio-cultural capital;
6. policies – that highlight the importance of racial parity, resource equity, and accountability for student success;
7. partnerships – focused on building a college prepared pipeline, professional opportunities, and facilitating fluid transitions between high school, college, and university life; and
8. inquiry – that is organized around a culture of critical analysis, responsibility for student outcomes, and organizational learning.

With respect to faculty members, several domains of institutional responsibility are relevant. Faculty (along with other institutional personnel) have responsibility for fostering affirming campus climates, culturally relevant practices, environments that promotes students' sense of belonging, support high impact engagement practices, and participating in a culture of critical analysis around student outcomes. In doing so, student success 'outcomes' (the 'O' in Wood and Palmer's model) are then actualized through a lens that acknowledges institutional responsibility and accountability.

While the theoretical notions (e.g., cognitive frames, C-A-O) espoused by Bensimon (2005) as well as Wood and Palmer (2014) lend useful conceptual understanding of the importance of an institutional responsibility perspective, empirical data also support these ideas. Through the CCSM, data have been collected on the experiences and outcomes of over 7,000 community college men. Research on factors that contribute to respondents' persistence, achievement (grades), action control (focus placed on school), and engagement with faculty members reveal a very clear pattern. This pattern prompted the authors to produce statistical models that predicted student success based on these outcomes.

The first model employed background factors (e.g., age, mother's highest level of education, father's highest level of education), defining factors (e.g., high school GPA, time status, total credits earned), and environmental pressures (e.g., hours work per week, number of financial dependents, total stressful life events). The second model employed faculty ethos measures indicating: (a) whether (based on students perceptions) faculty members made them feel like they belonged, (b) welcomed their engagement inside of class, (c) welcomed their engagement outside of class, and (d) communicated validating messages to them (e.g., "you belong", "you have the ability", "you can succeed"). In all cases, prediction models for Black and Latino males using students' background characteristics, defining factors, and environmental pressures accounted for only 10% of the variance in student success. In contrast, models including faculty ethos predicted 30% or more of the variance in student success.

More simply, this finding suggests that the ethos created by faculty members in class contributes significantly more to student success than students' characteristics and environmental pressures. In other words, student success is more of a function of the environments created by faculty members than factors relevant to students themselves. This point is salient, as it demonstrates faculty members' ability to support students in overcoming challenges, simply by being affirming, welcoming, and validating. Faculty members should view these results as empowering as they illustrate that the most critical determinants of success lie within *their* own influence of control. Other aspects of campus ethos are explored in the next section, in the context of the Socio-Ecological Outcomes (SEO) model.

Socio-Ecological Outcomes (SEO) Model

The primary theoretical framework undergirding this guidebook is the Socio-Ecological Outcomes (SEO) model. This model was developed based upon an extensive review of the published research on men of color in the community college. The model was also informed by scholarship on college men and masculinities, racial/identity development, student engagement, campus climates, and institutional responsibility research. The model adheres to a three-fold structure, including inputs, socio-ecological domains, and outcomes (see Figure 2).

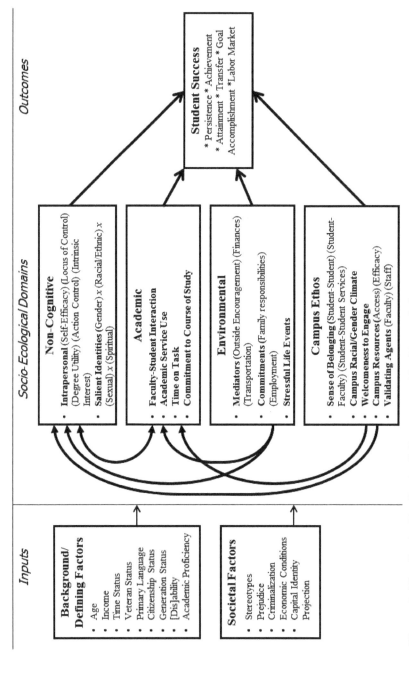

Figure 2. The Socio-Ecological Outcomes (SEO) model.

Inputs refer to factors that occur in students' lives prior to college that influence their experiences and interpretations of the collegiate environment. This is inclusive of background and defining factors, such as students' age, time status (e.g., part-time or full-time), veteran status, and ability status (among other factors). Essentially, these characteristics influence students' negotiation of college environments, representing important intersectionalities that must be taken into account when considering the diversity of men of color in college. Societal factors are inclusive of the social pressures that face men of color in wider society. It is well known that many men of color encounter stereotypes, prejudice, chronic financial challenges, and mass incarceration. Moreover, society has communicated messages to these men suggesting that they are not of worth and have not achieved success unless they have and can display their material wealth. Of course, given the economic challenges facing men of color, the resulting paradox is that some men of color will spend monies in ways that seem non-sensible (e.g., purchasing expensive rims, clothing, cars) because they have been socialized to believe that without these things, they are 'lesser than' (see Wood & Essien-Wood, 2012).

Collectively, the input factors shape the experiential realities of men of color in college. These experiences are filtered through four interrelated socio-ecological domains. The first domain encompasses *non-cognitive* factors relevant to students' intrapersonal lives and identities (e.g., gender, racial, spiritual). Intrapersonal factors are inclusive of affective, emotional, and dispositional responses to life pressures and the collegiate environment. This includes students': (a) self-efficacy – confidence in their ability to perform academically; (b) locus of control – feelings of control over their academic futures; (c) degree utility-perceived worthwhileness of their collegiate endeavors; (d) action control – focused attention towards academic matters; and (e) intrinsic interest – authentic interest in academic learning. To be clear, faculty members help shape these intrapersonal factors by building or negating students' confidence in themselves (self-efficacy), demonstrating the relevancy of academic learning to their lives and challenges they face (degree utility, intrinsic interest), and empowering them to take control over their academic careers (locus of control). Given the salience of these factors in the academic success of men of color, faculty should be thoughtful and intentional about communicating messages, structuring coursework, and delivering course content in a manner that builds healthy cognitive dispositions. The next chapter discusses this notion in more detail.

Also evident in the non-cognitive domain are identity factors relevant to students' gender, racial, and spiritual identities. While there are certainly more areas of identity (e.g., academic, class-based, ability status, sexual) that can directly influence success in college, these areas are generally the most relevant to men of color. Gender identity encompasses a number of factors, including whether men are comfortable seeking help, perceive school as a domain that men should engage, believe that school is a worthwhile endeavor in context of their roles as breadwinners, and have healthy understandings of competition in school contexts. Among these factors, comfort in seeking out help from faculty and staff is a particularly critical consideration. CCSM data indicate that 26% of Black and Latino men report that they are *not* comfortable seeking out help from faculty and staff. In fact, positive perceptions of help-seeking is *the* most strongest determinant of success for Latino men and the second strongest determinant for Black men.

Racial identity is most concerned with men's positive regard (perception) for their own ethnic communities. The nexus of the gender, racial, and spiritual identities further complicates the role of identity on student success. Identity is directly relevant to men's success in the classroom. For example, if men feel that by engaging in school they are negating their identities as 'people of color' and/or as 'men,' then they will be less likely to succeed. To be clear, discourse that is focused on the experiences of men of color in college that does not recognize their gendered identities fails to address a significant proportion of factors that influence their success.

The next domain addresses *academic* factors. These factors are typified by classic perceptions of student engagement, through faculty-student interactions in and out of the classroom, and use of campus services. In the context of this volume, faculty-student interactions are viewed as key to success for men of color. Data from the Beginning Postsecondary Students Longitudinal Study (BPS, 2009) has demonstrated that out-of-class interactions with faculty are key to success. BPS followed a cohort of first time students from the entry into college over the course of six years. Within this six year time frame, some students dropped out, some stopped out (left temporarily), and others completed their goals (attained a certificate, degree, or transferred). In six years, only 22.6% of Black men who 'never' talked with faculty members outside of class completed their goals. However, those who talked with faculty members 'sometimes,' completed their goals at a slightly higher rate, at 26.6%. Juxtaposed to these outcomes are data for Black men who reported talking with faculty members outside of class 'often.' For these men, 64.2% of them completed their goals in a six-year time frame. These data demonstrate the critical role that interactions with faculty have on student success. However, as evidenced earlier, these interactions are typically a function of a climate of 'welcomeness to engage' that faculty members create in and out of the classroom, as opposed to student characteristics and environmental pressures.

The third socio-ecological domain is focused on *environmental* considerations. Environmental factors are inclusive of the pressures that occur outside of college that can influence students' success inside of college. These pressures can include family commitments, work obligations, transportation issues, financial pressures, and experiences with stressful life events (e.g., divorce, incarceration, death in the family, loss of a job, eviction). With respect to employment, data examined via the CCSM has shown that men of color are concentrated in two categories, those who work full-time (36 hours or more) and those who do not work at all. The time spent working full-time can detract from students' focus on school. This may be one reason why social involvement (e.g., campus friendships, club/organization participation) tends to negatively influence student success for men of color. Specifically, social involvement coupled with external commitments (e.g., family, work) may detract the time students can dedicate towards academically successful habits (e.g., studying, attending class, using tutoring services).

Overall, environmental pressures are strong determinants of student success in college. In fact, research from Wood and Williams (2013) demonstrated that they could accurately predict whether a Black male community college student would persist through their first semester based solely on four environmental variables (e.g., hours worked per week, finances, life stress, and total dependents). It should be noted that environmental pressures influence student outcomes for other community college student groups as well, particularly underserved populations (e.g., low income, first-generation, students of color, part-timers). As a result, faculty should be knowledgeable of the environmental pressures facing men of color, as well as those facing other students.

Based upon the SEO model, it is postulated that environmental challenges have the most influence on student success through the non-cognitive and academic domains. In other words, environmental challenges affect students' confidence in their academic abilities (self-efficacy), detract from their focus on school (action control), and can limit the time necessary to engage with faculty and staff in meaningful ways. For example, a student who experiences numerous stressors in their life, is working full-time, and also trying to balance familial commitments who then performs poorly on a test or assignment may become more discouraged than a student without these pressures. For this student, the challenge of balancing their external life, coupled with some performance challenges, can reduce their confidence (self-efficacy) and make them question the utility of college (degree utility). Thus, the importance of building healthy non-cognitive outcomes in the classroom and providing structured methods of engagement are essential. In particular, faculty can foster positive non-cognitive outcomes that serve as protective mechanisms against student departure.

The final socio-ecological domain integrated in the SEO model is the campus ethos domain. The campus ethos domain addresses climate and cultural aspects of the college environment. Of all the domains discussed, this domain is perceived as having the most influence on student success, as a positive campus ethos can disrupt negative pressures on the academic and non-cognitive domains resulting from environmental pressures, societal factors, and background/defining characteristics. While there are several areas of focus in the campus ethos domain of importance to student success (i.e., campus climates that counter racial-gender based stereotypes, campus resources that are useful to resolving problems and accessible to students), the three most central elements of the domain include belonging, welcomeness to engage, and validation.

Sense of belonging is defined as, "students' perceived social support on campus, a feeling or sensation of connectedness, the experience of mattering or feeling cared about, accepted, respected, valued by, and important to the group (e.g., campus community) or others on campus (e.g., faculty, peers)" (Strayhorn, 2012, p. 3). Students who experience belonging will exhibit a greater commitment to college and, as a result, have an enhanced likelihood of success. Specifically, men of color need to perceive that faculty members care about their perspectives in class, value interacting with them during class, value their presence in class, care about their success, and believe they belong in class. In terms of a holistic class environment, it is also beneficial that students perceive a sense of belonging with other students as well.

Welcomeness to engage refers to the conditions created in and out of the classroom that communicate to students whether or not faculty members want students to engage with them. Thus, instead of being focused on whether or not a student asks questions in class, responds to questions in class, and inquires about their progress, faculty members should be more concerned with whether or not they have created conditions in the class where students feel welcome to ask questions, respond to questions, and inquire about their progress. Out of class, the same notions hold true. Students should also feel that faculty members welcome such interactions outside of class. Simple actions, such as smiling at students, saying hello, and waving at them on campus, can go a long way in fostering conditions that support engagement. Faculty can be even more proactive than this by purposively checking in on students (out of class) to see how they are doing academically and personally. The importance of welcomeness to engage is evidenced by Wood (2010). He found that men of color noted very few interactions with faculty outside of class. Students reported that, when faculty members saw them on campus, they walked the other direction, pretended to be on their phones, or acted occupied in ways that communicated that they did not want to interact with them. As a result, students noted that they were more likely to have meaningful and welcoming relationships with maintenance personnel, groundkeepers, and cafeteria workers than their faculty members.

Finally, validation is another key attribute of a positive campus ethos. According to Laura Rendón (1994), "validation is an enabling, confirming and supportive process initiated by in- and out-of-class agents that fosters academic and interpersonal development" (p. 44). Validation is often communicated from campus personnel (e.g., faculty, staff) to students through messages that suggest that, "you have the ability to do the work," "you can succeed," "you belong here," and "I believe in you." Validation is critical to success for men of color in college. In fact, in CCSM statistical models, validation from faculty is the third strongest determinant of achievement (grades) for Black men. Unfortunately, too often, men as a whole do not receive these messages from faculty. In fact, data from the CCSM indicate that half of college men (across racial/ethnic groups) receive no validation at all from faculty members. While this is a very concerning pattern for men as a whole, given the intensified pressures facing many men of color, these messages are even more critical for their continuation and success in college.

This chapter has sought to provide a contextual foundation for the promising practices discussed in this guidebook. The authors have overviewed factors necessitating enhanced teaching and learning strategies, the institutional responsibility perspective on student success, and the Socio-Ecological Outcomes (SEO) model that guided inquiry reported in this volume. Hopefully, readers have come to a realization that enhanced strategies for men of color are necessary due to their experiences with external pressures, racial-gender stereotypes, inadequate preparation for collegiate work, and male gender socialization. The next chapter begins this guidebook's treatment of promising practices for men of color by focusing on relational strategies.

PART II

BUILDING RELATIONSHIPS WITH
MEN OF COLOR

Given the challenges and social pressures discussed in the previous section of this guidebook, enhanced teaching and learning strategies that facilitate student success for men of color in community colleges are necessary to address persistent outcome gaps and disparities. As noted, classroom faculty in community colleges have both an opportunity and an obligation to create and sustain conditions that effectively engage men of color in the learning context, build confidence, increase self-efficacy, and enable men of color to assume ownership of their learning experiences and outcomes. While it is both easy and reasonable to focus exclusively on the pedagogical strategies that are employed by faculty in teaching and facilitating student learning, findings from data collected via the CCSM and faculty leaders underscore the relational component of teaching and the critical role it plays in the learning experiences of men of color in community colleges. Thus, the purpose of this section of the guidebook is to present and discuss effective practices that can be utilized by faculty in building relationships with men of color. Faculty who are able to seamlessly integrate these practices will likely build greater rapport with men of color in their classes and, as a result, observe greater levels of engagement, persistence, and achievement among these students.

Dispositions Fostered by Enhanced Relationships

Gardenhire-Crooks, Collado, Martin, and Castro (2010) confirm that a critical mass of men of color who are enrolled in community colleges had K-12 schooling experiences that were less than desirable. These experiences were typified by low expectations from teachers and negative stereotypes about them due to their racial/ethnic and gender affiliation. Consequently, some of these students matriculate to college with negative dispositions and attitudes toward schooling. Others anticipate relationships with educators that are rooted in adversity or indifference. These concerns are in essence confirmed when students perceive faculty as unwelcoming, racially prejudice, or uncaring.

Conversely, enhanced relationships between faculty and men of color engender positive attitudes about schooling among students, which has been associated with a host of desirable academic and psychosocial outcomes. CCSM findings confirm that men who report healthy relationships with faculty also report greater feelings of belonging and connectedness to the campus. Moreover, these men are also more likely to seek help from faculty to resolve academic and personal problems, have a greater sense of confidence in their academic abilities, and report being more focused in school. The significance of enhanced relationships between faculty and men of color was also a salient theme in the data that were collected from faculty leaders. These findings, as well as those reported in the published literature on men of color in community colleges demonstrate that relational dynamics in the teaching and learning process serve as the foundation of students' experiences and success. Stated simply, regardless of how skillful faculty members may be in teaching content, men of color are not likely to be successful in their courses in the absence of relationships that are rooted in trust, mutual respect, and authentic care. As one of the faculty leaders indicated:

> Anyone can teach skills and strategies to success. What makes my approach unique is that I go beyond providing classroom skills and techniques to be successful. My approach to teaching starts with the student; looking at self and how choices, thoughts, and behavior positively or negative influence the outcomes of their goals and dreams.

Our assertions regarding enhanced relationships as a foundational precursor to effective teaching and learning for men of color are depicted in the "Pyramid of Student Success" presented in Figure 3. Situated at the very bottom (or foundation of the pyramid) is the relational dynamic of teaching and learning, which encompasses trust, mutual respect, and authentic care from faculty. Upon the relational dynamic rest effective and engaging pedagogy, which are integral to student success but cannot have its desired impact in the absence of enhanced relationships. Finally, at the apex of the pyramid is student success, which is achieved when effective pedagogy and enhanced relationships are seamlessly integrated in the teaching and learning context.

Having discussed the critical role that enhanced relationships with faculty play in serving as a pre-condition to student success for men of color, the remainder of this section will focus on steps and strategies that faculty can enact to foster these relationships with students. While our focus in this guidebook is on strategies that are especially salient for men of color in community colleges, some may find that many of these strategies are transferable to other student populations as well. The efficacy of these strategies for men of color is elevated by the challenges and social pressures presented in Part I of the guidebook, which are reportedly experienced by a preponderance of these students in community colleges. We contend that enhanced relationships (coupled with effective and engaging pedagogy) play an important role in mediating the effects of external pressures, racial-gender stereotypes, male gender role socialization, and academic preparation issues that contaminate the experiences and compromise success for men of color in community colleges.

Figure 3. Pyramid of Student Success for Men of Color in Community Colleges.

Relationship-Building Strategies

As noted previously, strategies presented in this guidebook were derived from several sources, including: an exhaustive review of published research on men of color, narratives and interviews with men of color, data from the Community College Survey of Men, and insights derived from faculty leaders. Analyses of the data and published literature yielded ten strategies that can be employed by faculty to establish and foster relationships with men of color that are conducive to their success in community college. These strategies were clustered into three overarching categories, which included: (1) positive messaging, (2) authentic care, and (3) intrusive interventions. Essentially, these practices fostered a sense of belonging, validation, and the belief that faculty care about and are invested in the success of men of color.

Some educators may understandably question if this type of support is going beyond what is necessary and appropriate for college students. To that concern, we contend that men of color in community colleges often need this type of support due to negative experiences in preK-12 schooling, racial prejudice, societal messages that convey to them that they are not capable of being successful in school, and academic learning that is not aligned with socially constructed notions of masculinity. Thus, community college faculty are uniquely-positioned to counter perceptions of school and to resituate learning in a manner that addresses the lived socio-cultural realities and identities of men of color. Also, given that community colleges are typically open-access institutions, faculty should anticipate that some students will need attention and support that goes beyond what is expected at a university or more selective institutions. Toward this end, faculty leaders offered insights for relationship and rapport building strategies that could be employed to facilitate student success for men of color.

Positive Messaging

Strategies that are presented in the positive messaging category help to challenge or offset discouraging and deficit-oriented discourse that have been directed towards men of color. This discourse can come from many individuals, including K-12 teachers, counselors, school administrators and other educators who were not committed to their success and/or did not believe they were capable of learning due to racist assumptions and stereotypes. While men of color who are enrolled in community colleges may not have experienced these barriers, published literature and research on the experiences of young boys of color in K-12 schools suggest that many have. Consequently, despite their willingness and motivation to purse postsecondary education, some men of color have internalized the belief that school is not a place where they belong and is not conducive to their success. Thus, community college faculty must be mindful that men of color who are enrolled in their classes may be reluctant to engage or fully participate in class discussions due to reticence about their belonging at the institution. Even those who believe they belong may be reluctant to fully engage because they assume others in the class setting, notably peers, question their presence.

Men of color's engagement in class may also be stifled by gender-based assumptions that school is a feminine space. As such, some may perceive that men who participate fully or enthusiastically are somehow going against established norms and expectations for men. The confluence of these and other racialized assumptions about the presence and capabilities of men of color in education necessitates effort on the part of faculty to help men unlearn and reject myths and stereotypes about them. Community college faculty should consider the following practices in their efforts to convey positive messages about education to men of color and engender a sense of belonging in community college for these students.

Create an Environment that Welcomes Engagement

As discussed in the overview of the SEO model, faculty members must work arduously to foster an environment where students feel welcome to engage. A perception of welcomeness to engage is foundational to effect positive messaging, as it serves to foreground subsequent communication from faculty to students. In this light, nonverbal communication may be more critical to fostering conditions for welcomeness than what is said. As such, faculty members should demonstrate, via their body language, eye contact, active listening, and general demeanor that they want students to engage with them formally and informally. This is a critical point, as students can often make assessments about faculty care and concern for them without ever speaking with them. As such, positive messaging to men of color begins with intentional nonverbal communication that is inviting and affirming. Verbal communication is also critical to positive messaging about school. Sometimes, what is said to men of color is less important than *how* it is communicated. Vocal intonation, non-defensive language, and repetition of ideas and concerns expressed by men are some, among many, positive messaging approaches.

Criticize Privately, Praise Publicly

Given the concerns that many men of color have about actualizing stereotypes regarding their inferiority, it is essential that faculty members provide critiques of their performance in personal settings. For example, faculty members should avoid (with all purposefulness) any public critique of men of color relevant to their academic performance. Thus, concerns about responses given in class discussion, coursework performance, the efficacy of work done in groups, or missing assignments should be addressed one-on-one. When addressing concerns, faculty should provide honest assessments of students' skills and abilities. This will ensure that students do not falsely believe that they are performing well in class, only to receive poor marks at the end of the course. Providing honest feedback can be difficult, especially in rare cases when levels of performance are strikingly low. In such circumstances, communicating feedback in a manner that demonstrates care for students and allows them to maintain their personal dignity is critical.

Faculty can pull students aside before or after class or communicate with them via email about the need to meet in person to discuss issues. This approach can reduce students' anxiety about race-based stereotypes, which suggest that students of color are not intellectual. Moreover, given that men seek pride and a sense of control in academic and non-academic settings, private critiques can avoid emasculating men of color (Sáenz, Bukoski, Lu, & Rodriguez, 2013). Faculty leaders noted that faculty members should publically highlight the success of men of color in the classroom. This approach benefits men of color by increasing their self-confidence, but also serves to demonstrate to other students in the class that men of color are capable of performing at high academic levels. Such messaging can serve to deconstruct stereotypical notions about the abilities of men of color, both for themselves and for other students. The crux of public praise is that it should be authentic and provided only for meaningful and insightful contributions. In other words, if faculty are perceived as providing undue praise or trying to portray small contributions as being larger than they actually are, then public praise can have the opposite effect as intended.

Increase Validation and Sense of Belonging

Creating a climate of validation and belonging in the classroom is an integral component to student success for men of color. Validation entails communicating (both verbally and non-verbally) that faculty believe in students' ability to succeed and their ability to do college-level work. Communication of these messages inside and outside of class, and in one-on-one and group settings, is key to effectively validating men of color. Validation empowers students to perform at high levels, and has been shown through CCSM data to enhance men's confidence, focus in school, authentic interest in learning, and perceptions of the value of a college degree. Faculty members who validate students can foster increased perceptions of belonging in college. Some indicators of students' perceptions of belonging include assessments that faculty members care about their success, value interactions with them, value their presence, and believe that they belong in school.

To achieve these indicators, faculty must regularly communicate high expectations, demonstrate care for students' academic well-being, and their authentic interest in the student as a person. Examples of validating communication include: "I'm glad you're here," "what a powerful essay," "you are really good at this," "wonderful job, do you mind if I show this to others as an example?," and "I feel so fortunate to have you in class." A key determinant of the effectiveness of validation is the authenticity of the message conveyed. Men of color are highly adept at evaluating the legitimacy and genuineness of messages. This may be especially true when being validated, as these men may have *very* limited experience in being affirmed in academic contexts. Thus, the messages rendered from faculty to students are often filtered through the lens of prior messages from faculty, as well as social expectations of being people of color and men.

Avoid Unintentional Micromessaging Regarding
Misconceptions about Men of Color

Faculty can unintentionally invalidate students when they are seeking to validate them. For example, men of color often experience racial and gender microaggressions in community college settings. Microaggressions are, "brief and commonplace daily verbal, behavioral, or environmental indignities, whether intentional or unintentional, that communicate hostile, derogatory, or negative racial slights and insults towards people of color" (Sue et al., 2007, p. 271). Often, microaggressions are unintentionally and unknowingly communicated to men of color. There are several primary types of unconsciously communicated microaggressions that have been identified, such as microinsults, microinvalidations, and microexclusions (Essien-Wood, 2010). Microinsults are comments that degrade a person based on their identity (Sue et al., 2007). Examples of microinsults include messages that communicate a sense of surprise about a student's academic abilities, such as "wow, you are very articulate," "huh, you are really good at math," or "great response." Seemingly, such comments could be construed as compliments; but when said in a manner that demonstrates surprise about a student's ability, these messages are demeaning. Other common examples of microinsults involve assumptions of criminality, in which faculty members avoid men of color on campus at night, unduly monitor them for cheating, or avoid meeting with them one-on-one for fear of them. Unfortunately, research from Gardenhire-Crooks et al. (2010) demonstrates that men of color have experiences in community colleges. They found that Black, Latino, and Native American men, "routinely experienced stereotypical attitudes that linked them to thuggery and violence, among many other negative associations," as their, "very existence made them suspect in the eyes of some" (p. 21).

Microinvalidations are another form of microaggression. These microaggressions invalidate the thoughts, perspectives, and experiences of students (Sue et al., 2007). Examples of microinvalidations include a faculty member asking a male of color whether they are a second language learner, negating their experiences with racisms as over-attributing 'everything' to race, or assuming that their experiences with marginalization equate with those of men of color. Microexclusions represent an additional microaggression domain. Microexclusions involve ignoring, leaving out, and allowing people of color to be made invisible (Essien-Wood, 2010). Microexclusions can occur in numerous contexts, but in the classroom they are often presented through excluding men of color in group selection, not calling on men of color during discussions, setting up the physical classroom space to segregate certain students, and forgetting about whether or not a male of color attended class. Such actions (though likely unintentional) can serve to foster an environment of alienation and isolation.

Authentic Care

As noted several times in this guidebook, many men of color in community colleges have not enjoyed positive relationships with teachers and other educators in their prior schooling experiences. Such experiences can make students view faculty as 'threats' as opposed to 'supports.' When this occurs, students are less likely to attend office hours, participate in class discussions, and prioritize the course in light of other challenges and demands. In contrast, prior research has demonstrated the manifold benefits experienced by students when they perceive that faculty members authentically care about them and their success. For example, via interviews conducted with Black men at a southwestern community college, Wood and Turner (2011) found that perceiving faculty members as 'friendly and caring' was a strong contributor to the persistence and academic achievement of these male collegians. Overwhelmingly, findings from the faculty leaders study also conveyed the important role and benefits of routinely and authentically communicating care for students and their well-being. For example, one faculty leader stated the following:

> Caring about student persistence and success through regular consistent engagement and feedback is another key component. This includes, but is not limited to, acknowledging students' humanity with respect and an on-going supportive attitude. For many of my students, just noticing differences in their presence, demeanor, and behavior (positive, negative or changed) solicits a greater willingness to communicate what's going on with them and trust in me, which also increases their willingness to address whatever stresses, situations, or distractions are impacting their ability to focus. This is particularly true when it is apparent they are overwhelmed. It could mean the difference between them giving up or finding the tenacity to make it through the challenge and/or fear they're facing. Caring really does count!

Results from the Community College Survey of Men affirm the salience of the above quote. Specifically, findings from this survey confirm that authentic care produces manifold benefits for Black, Mexicano, Latino, and Southeast Asian men. Predictive analyses illustrated that students' perceptions of authentic care from faculty were determinants of increased focus on academic matters, authentic interest in course learning, and confidence in students' academic abilities. Data from this survey has also shown that authentic care is associated with healthy masculine dispositions. Specifically, men who perceived that faculty members cared about them and their success had a greater willingness to seek out academic and personal support, as well as to perceive school as a domain equally suited for the success of both men and women. In light of these benefits, presented below are a set of promising practices for cultivating relationships that are rooted in authentic care between men of color and community college faculty.

Arrive a Few Minutes Early and Leave a Few
Minutes Late

While validation is integral to fostering a sense of belonging, simpler interactions can also create an environment of belonging. For example, faculty members can make a point to warmly greet students as they enter the classroom. This of course would require faculty members to arrive a few minutes early; yet such action can go a long way in fostering an environment of inclusion. For example, faculty can say hello, make friendly eye contact, and smile at students as they enter the class. As such, faculty should avoid asking students difficult questions or engaging in other actions that would detract students from arriving to class early. While these actions may seem trite, they position students as having a valued place in the classroom. If a faculty member enters class after some students have arrived, he or she can take a few moments to check in with each student. In like manner, faculty should also leave class a few minutes later. Doing so may provide a space for faculty to have short interactions with students as they leave class. As students are leaving, faculty can make comments such as, "glad you were here," "great contributions today," "thanks for speaking up," and "I appreciate your commitment to this course." Moreover, they can ask questions such as, "how are you doing with material?", "how are your other classes going?", and "is this course content useful to what you're doing out of class?".

Connect with Students as Individuals

Connecting with students on a personal level is another essential element to effectively establishing relationships with men of color. Getting to know students on a personal level will often entail conversations that fall outside the normal academic discourse about grades, course performance, and major choice. Instead, personal conversations should focus on the student as a unique individual who is worthy of the faculty member's attention. However, these conversations can also help faculty troubleshoot challenges students may be facing. This is especially important given that Black men have 130% greater odds of leaving college within three years of enrollment due to personal reasons (in comparison to their male peers) (Wood, 2012c). This can be inclusive of informal conversations about personal matters and pressures, social interests, and goal aspirations. Personal matters and pressures entail conversations about familial matters, work obligation, dependents, and other external factors that can support and pull students away from their focus on school. Social interests involve conversations that address popular topics around sports, news, and entertainment. Faculty can also speak with students about their goal aspirations. This can be inclusive of major, career, and community-centric goals. Research from Wood and Palmer (2012) demonstrate that men of color have varying goals when they enter college. They employed national data to examine how Black men's goals compared to that of their ethnic peers. Their findings indicated that Black men were more likely to desire to be community leaders and be financially secure. Whereas, Latino men had greater desires to maintain close familial ties by living near relatives. In contrast, White men placed a higher value on necessary personal and leisure time. These differences are not unsubstantial, and represent a few of many areas of life aspirations and goals that faculty can discuss with students. While engaging with men of color is essential to their success, it is important that faculty members do so cautiously. Faculty should be careful not to stereotype men of color and assume that they all think about and like the same things. For example, conversations that immediately focus on athletics or hip-hop, or assume a common political ideology can be off-putting (even in circumstances where such interests are valid). Additionally, faculty members should keep an open mind with students, not judging them for their appearance, experiences, or viewpoints.

Be Willing to Engage Men Out of Class

Faculty leaders discussed the importance of both in-class and out-of-class interactions with men of color. While much of this guidebook addresses in-class interactions, it is imperative that faculty recognize the intensified benefit of out-of-class interactions for men of color. As noted earlier in this guidebook, of the Black men who reported interacting with faculty members out-of-class 'often,' 64.2% completed their goals in six-years. Thus, faculty should welcome opportunities to engage with students formally and informally out-of-class. In particular, it is paramount that faculty members do not treat men of color as if they are invisible out of class. If a faculty member is walking on campus and sees a recognizable student face, he or she should smile, wave at them, say hello, and talk with them about non-academic matters (e.g., news, plans for the weekend). If a conversation transitions from a short exchange to a discussion about academic matters and academic support, then faculty members should demonstrate their welcoming of such interactions. In the extreme, some faculty respondents noted that they made it a point to workout at the same campus gym as students. They noted that this enabled students to see them in a more personal light and to demystify the artificial barriers that exist between faculty and students. While not all faculty can make such commitments, being creative about fostering out-of-class interactions should be of core concern for faculty members who teach men of color.

Intrusive Interventions

Consistently communicating positive messages about men of color's abilities to be successful and conveying authentic care about their well-being and success are necessary, yet insufficient on their own. Faculty leaders in the study confirm that community college faculty must also be willing and prepared to intervene intrusively when they see men of color struggling or falling through the cracks. This is especially important in light of CCSM findings about men of color's reluctance to seek help for personal and academic problems. As noted previously, nearly 26% of Black and Latino men indicated that they are not comfortable seeking help from campus personnel when they need it. Given this, community college faculty can ill afford to wait for men of color to approach them or seek them out for support. Thus, faculty must be proactive in their efforts to support these students. It is likely that some men of color will not respond enthusiastically to initial efforts from faculty who offer support. Yet, faculty should not be discouraged by students who are not responsive at the outset. Some students may be skeptical to unsolicited support from faculty because they have never experienced or observed it from educators in their prior schooling. Others may be embarrassed or ashamed to accept support because it entails admitting that they need help to be successful. These and other similar reasons, notwithstanding persistence from faculty, are necessary to ensure success for these students. Below are two intrusive intervention strategies faculty can employ to support men of color who appear to be struggling in their courses.

Avoid the "Approach Me First" and "Prove Yourself First" Stances

Faculty leaders expressed the importance of engaging students in positive and affirming relationships. They noted that communication with men of color was a key component of successful teaching and learning. Notwithstanding, while faculty leaders extolled the importance of relationships with students, research on men of color in community colleges demonstrates that this does not always occur. Specifically, Wood (2014) conducted interviews with Black men at a community college in the southwestern United States. The focus of this study was to better understand factors that influence the success of Black men in college. Students attributed interactions with faculty as a key determinant of their success. However, many students noted being apprehensive to engage in the classroom for fear that faculty would perceive them as academically inferior. Therefore, students avoided raising their hands, responding to questions, participating in group work, or attending office hours because they perceived that doing so would lead to faculty members viewing them as unintelligent.

However, students noted that faculty viewed their apprehension to engage as apathy toward their academic pursuits. As a result, faculty employed an "approach me first" or "prove yourself first" stance. In this light, students had to initiate the first interactions with faculty and demonstrate their interest in and commitment to the course before faculty members would reciprocate their interest in the student. In other words, student engagement served as a trigger for faculty members' reciprocation of that engagement. As noted by Wood (2014), the confluence of students' 'apprehension to engage' with the 'approach me first' and 'prove yourself first' stance, "created a perfect storm that never provided an opportunity for faculty or students to engage one another in- and out-of the classroom" (p. 795). Given this, Wood asserted that faculty members should be proactive in engaging students in the classroom by initiating interactions and avoiding actions that require students to approach them and prove their commitments first. Now, given the high number of students taught by faculty members, initiating engagement with all students may be difficult to do. This challenge may be especially acute for part-time faculty who teach at multiple campuses with limited time at each site. However, faculty-student relationships (as demonstrated through this guidebook) are critical to the success of men of color and have an intensified benefit for their success. Thus, creating meaningful and intentional interactions with students should be prioritized.

Check in Frequently with Students—Especially
Those Who "Disappear" for a Period of Time

Checking in with students on a regular basis is one way that faculty can be proactive in reaching out and supporting students. Findings from the CCSM confirm that routine check-ins from faculty have a positive influence on key indicators of student success for men of color, notably engagement with faculty during class, self-efficacy, confidence in their abilities to be successful, and use of campus services (to name a few). Participants in the faculty leaders study also underscored the importance of checking in with men of color on a regular basis—citing it as one of several strategies faculty can employ to convey to students a sense of care and concern. Faculty who teach at campuses that utilize early alert systems can automate their check-ins by sending alerts to students as necessary. However, check-ins need not be as formal or elaborate as an early alert system. Email messages, text messages, and phone calls can go a long way toward reaching out to men of color proactively. In doing so, faculty can convey to students that they are "concerned about their progress in the course," or "noticed they did not do as well as expected on an assignment and welcome an opportunity to discuss how their performance could be improved."

As noted previously, some men of color may not be immediately responsive to these efforts from faculty. Nevertheless, they are critically important and can be the difference between students persisting or withdrawing from a course. Faculty should not be only compelled to check in with men of color who are struggling, but also with students whose performance in the course is 'satisfactory' or even 'excellent.'

Faculty should also consider checking in with students who attended classes regularly, but abruptly stopped attending for a period of time. Some students may have experienced a personal issue that has impacted their ability to attend class. Faculty may be positioned to assist the student by directing him to campus support services or resources that may be useful in helping him resolve the issue and return to classes. Regardless of the reasons that prompt faculty to check-in, doing so conveys to men of color a sense of validation, care, and visibility that many have not have experienced at any point during their schooling.

Avoid Simply Directing Students to Support Resources - Facilitate a Connection with a Colleague

While it is important for faculty to be knowledgeable about the range and efficacy of campus support services that are available to facilitate student success in their courses, getting men of color to utilize these services is critical. As we have noted several times throughout this guidebook, being willing to seek help with personal or academic problems is a key correlate of success for men of color in community colleges. However, traditional patterns of gender socialization often serve as barriers to doing so. Thus, faculty who are committed to ensuring men of color's success in their classes must not only direct students to appropriate support services, but should also be intrusive and assertive in guiding their use of the services. Common practices for informing students of support services—such as listing them in course syllabi and announcing them during the first day of classes are worthwhile first steps. When referring men of color to these services, faculty should consider taking some additional steps, such as facilitating connections with colleagues who oversee these services or even accompanying these students to their initial visits to the offices where services are offered—particularly those services that can be negatively stigmatized, such as student counseling and disability support services. Faculty who take the time to enact these additional steps not only signal to students the importance of these services, but also a genuine concern for their well-being, which can have a positive impact on their persistence in community college.

Holistically, the strategies and approaches outlined in this chapter served to foster positive relationships between men of color and faculty. As noted throughout this chapter, these relationships are an integral foundation to student success for these men. In the next chapter, we discuss promising teaching practices that, when coupled with positive and affirming relationships, can serve to advance the learning and success of men of color in community colleges.

PART III

PROMISING TEACHING PRACTICES

While relationships with men of color are integral to laying a stable foundation for learning, effective teaching practices are necessary to advance course content knowledge. The focus of this chapter is to explicate promising teaching practices that were identified by faculty leaders. The attitudinal perspective necessary for establishing and maintaining effective relationships with men of color are also necessary for the effective delivery of course content. To be clear, faculty members must communicate to men of color that they are worthy of investment, are believed in, and are critical to the classroom learning environment. These messages, while important for all students, are critical to success for men of color. Specifically, men of color experience an intensified benefit from such messaging due to external pressures in their lives (e.g., familial responsibilities, work commitments, stressful life events), preK-12 experiences of classroom marginalization, and the socialization of men of color in wider society to perceive academics as being counter to their identities. When life barriers are effectively countered in the classroom with effective messaging, men of color can become empowered to overcome challenges they face in class and in society.

Dispositions Fostered by Promising Practices

In the context of teaching, faculty leaders argued that promising teaching practices for men of color should foster empowerment, inculcate help-seeking, and demystify perceptions of school as a feminine domain. Among these dispositions, the notion of empowerment was the most central theme embodied within the recommendations for teaching practice. Faculty leaders noted that promising teaching practices should empower men of color to become increasingly resilient to the multitude of pressures facing them in their lives. In this light, positive faculty attitudes about men of color and their abilities serve as a core coping mechanism to overcome the economic, political, and social challenges they encounter. According to faculty leaders in the study, empowering teaching practices avoids a cultural deficit perspective that blames students, their families, and their communities for deleterious school outcomes. Instead, a focus is placed on the power within students, their peers, families, and communities to succeed personally and to change systems and processes that disadvantage others like them.

Beyond empowerment, faculty leaders were overwhelmingly attentive to the intersections of race/ethnicity and gender. They noted that promising teaching practices encompassed approaches that foster help-seeking and perceptions of school as a domain that is equally suited for men and women. With respect to the prior (help-seeking), faculty leaders noted that men of color may be less likely to seek out help due to stereotypes in wider society, which suggest that they are unintelligent and indolent. As such, many men of color will avoid asking a faculty member for help in class, going to their office hours, or asking questions in class for fear of actualizing stereotypes about them[1]. Moreover, this apprehension to engage is coupled with traditional masculine scripts that suggest that men who seek out help are weak, feminine, and inferior. These notions of race and gender, coupled together, prompted many faculty leaders to recommend strategies that foster help-seeking and provide safe spaces for doing so.

Demystifying the notion of school as a domain solely suited for women (particularly White women) was also addressed by faculty leaders. Prior to entering college, boys and young men of color are overwhelmingly educated by White female teachers. In fact, 85% of the K-12 teacher workforce is comprised of White women (Feistritzer, 2011). From early on in their schooling process, these males are taught, based upon the demographic composition of the teaching force, that school is suited for women, not men. Therefore, when a young boy of color engages in school, he may be ridiculed and dismissed by others as being 'feminine' (Harris & Harper, 2008). Therefore, the collective preponderance of the messages received from peers, on television, from family, and the demographic makeup of teachers can socialize males of color to avoid engagement in school. This is similar to the experiences of many students of color who are taught early on, based on societal messages and teacher demographics, that school is not suited for them, but is designed to serve White children. The

---

[1] See Claude Steele's (1997; 1999) work on 'stereotype threat' as well as Wood's (2014) research on 'apprehension to engage'.

confluence of these two messages ("school is for Whites" and "school is for girls") is intensified for boys of color who are affected negatively by both sets of messaging. Therefore, faculty leaders in this study suggested that effective college teaching worked to challenge stereotypes about school by encouraging men, particularly men of color, to see school as a site where they belong.

Promising Teaching Practices

The teaching practices identified during the faculty study were clustered into four primary strategy areas, including: (1) content relevancy, (2) critical reflection, (3) collaborative learning, and (4) performance monitoring. Holistically, these areas widely encompass promising practices embodied within culturally relevant teaching. This pedagogical approach has been espoused by critical educators for years as an effective mechanism for teaching and working with disadvantaged communities. While similar to the notions of culturally "inclusive,' 'responsive,' 'congruent,' 'compatible,' and 'appropriate' pedagogies, culturally relevant pedagogy succeeds in taking into account both the micro and macro social-cultural and political context in which students are educated (Ladson-Billings, 1995). Within this perspective, culturally relevant teaching is, "a pedagogy that empowers students intellectually, socially, emotionally, and politically by using cultural referents to impart knowledge, skills, and attitudes" (Ladson-Billings, 1992, p. 382). Culturally relevant pedagogy, while very useful as a framework for teaching students of color, has not been as widely applied for teaching male students of color. As such, masculine identity must be intentionally recognized as a socio-cultural referent from which knowledge, skills, and attitudes specific to men of color must be embedded into teaching practices. What follows, is an explication of promising teaching practices intentionally focused on educating men of color.

Relevant Content

The most recurrent theme expressed by faculty was the need to incorporate culturally relevant content in the classroom. Ensuring that course content is relevant to the lives and experiences of men of color is a critical component of effective teaching. In general, this approach is an important factor in the learning of men of color. Content relevant to their lives will help keep men of color focused on lessons and assignments, involved in discussions, and critically reflective upon the importance of their role in society and school. Faculty leaders noted that employing culturally relevant content can increase students' confidence in their academic abilities (self-efficacy), imbue respect for multiple viewpoints, and increase students' authentic interest in academic content (intrinsic interest). All courses, regardless of topical area (e.g., economics, political science, biology), can employ academic content that intentionally incorporates the contributions of diverse groups into course lectures in a meaningful way. Below are some suggestions for embedding culturally relevant content into course lectures.

Use Historical Content That Demonstrates How
Course Concepts, Ideas, Theories, and
Applications Were Informed by People of Diverse
Racial/Ethnic and Gender Backgrounds

Numerous historical figures across academic disciplines were men of color. These men include inventors, philosophers, scientists, and social scientists who contributed to important technological and ideological advances. For example, key figures include: Frederick Douglas, W.E.B. Dubois, Charles Drew, Elijah McCoy, George Washington Carver, Lewis Latimer, Percy Julian, Benjamin Banneker, Granville Woods (among many others). Often, the incorporation of men of color in society is limited to ethnic specific courses. As a result, a lion share of students who do not have the opportunity to take these courses may not be exposed to the historical contributions of their racial/ethnic community to wider society. When the roles and lives of people of color are acknowledged, their incorporation is typically limited to slavery and the Civil Rights Movement. As noted by one faculty leader in the study, "by giving the student more events to use in context, it allows for higher and more effective learning and a better appreciation of the role they place in society." Thus, faculty should be intentional about addressing the contributions of men of color while laying historical foundations for contemporary topics in class. In particular, showing images of these men can enable men of color to visually see the academic content as being relevant to them.

Connect Rigorous Course Content to Themes
That are Relevant to the Lives, Issues, and
Experiences of Men of Color

While it is essential that faculty foreground topical content in a historical context that acknowledges the role of men of color, it is also essential that men of color see how this content addresses their current lives. As a result, faculty members should connect course content to contemporary topics (e.g., technology, pop culture, current events) in the lives of men of color. Course content should be directly applicable to the 'real life' experiences of men of color in the context of work, family, and friendships (among other areas). Class readings, assignments (e.g., essays, research papers, presentations), and lectures should provide opportunities for students to make explicit linkages between what they are learning in class and their lives. This approach will better enable students to interrogate misinformation and to recognize how the information they are learning can lead to a better life for themselves and their families. In making content relevant to daily life, faculty members should:

- Emphasize contemporary examples of the success of men of color in business, medical research, and technology.
- Underscore accomplishments of men of color in pursuits not traditionally highlighted in wider society. For instance, while faculty can employ examples from sports and entertainment, they should avoid doing so excessively.
- Discuss how current legal and political events can directly affect men of color both positively and negatively.

- Provide examples of how course content applies to life challenges such as financial barriers, stress, and the criminal justice system (See Terry, 2010 for an excellent example of this approach).

Using these strategies is essential, especially during the transition into college. As noted by one faculty leader, "once they can begin to bridge the gap between academics and their community, the transition to college is much smoother." As noted earlier, effective teaching practices serve to empower men of color. As such, faculty members should connect course content to their lives in a manner that allows men of color to consider, engage, and resolve issues that arise in their lives.

Employ Content That Expresses Differing
Viewpoints on the Same Topic

In a course where there are numerous topics to cover and too little time to cover them, information can be presented in a uni-dimensional fashion. When this occurs, students may be inadvertently educated to believe that there is a single, myopic way to view information that may be, in fact, multidimensional in nature. This approach may be exacerbated by teaching practices in preK-12 that adhere to a culture of 'only one way' that is fostered by the proliferation of standardized testing. As a result, faculty leaders recommended that effective content should acknowledge multiple worldviews, perspectives, and ideologies. In particular, recognition of the role of culturally situated vantage points is necessary. One strategy of accomplishing this goal is to provide multiple readings on the same topic, which allows students to see how differing life experiences and social realities can influence personal perspectives. Focus should be placed on both the perspective expressed and *why* the perspective has salience for the individual expressing it. Doing so can increase students' critical thinking skills and foster appreciation for social, cultural, and personal differences. In addition, this approach can enable men of color to understand the validity of *their* personal perspectives. In particular, readings from other men of color or those who have experienced (and overcame) life struggles can further empower students to make direct connections between course content and their daily lives.

Suggestion: The notion of having multiple viewpoints on one topic can also be extended to assignments. Consider encouraging students to think about different ways in which they can complete course assignments. Typically, assignments allow for some degree of flexibility in terms of topical area addressed, format, or style. Empower students to address the assignment guidelines while also making it applicable to their lives, personal interests, and to broaden their knowledge base.

Feature Diverse Guest Speakers and Lecturers
Who Can Address Varied Topics

Some faculty use guest speakers and lecturers as a strategy to convey course material. Guest speakers can come from a variety of backgrounds, but are typically professionals in the field or other faculty members. Generally, guest speakers and lecturers have extensive expertise in a specific topical area and can share unique insights relevant to their expertise with students. Guest speakers represent a key demographic that faculty can use to enhance the relevancy of their content for men of color. As such, faculty members should be intentional about which guest speakers they feature in class. As noted earlier, the vast majority of preK-12 teachers are White and female. While the gender composition of faculty is more equitably distributed in community college, 83% of these faculty are White (AACC, 2014). Guest speakers who represent diverse racial/ethnic, cultural, and gender communities should be prioritized. In particular, guest speakers who are both successful professionals in the field and men of color should be sought. These speakers can simultaneously shed light on specific topical areas of interest while enabling students to envision themselves in careers of interest. Given the demographic makeup of community college faculty, it is critical that students see individuals in their field of interest who are (in some way) reflective of them. In particular, having guest speakers discuss their work lives and highlight the obstacles they overcame to reach their goals is critical. Some faculty leaders in the study also recommended inviting former male of color students to serve as guest speakers. They noted that such guests can serve as strong, "role models and mentors for the younger men in the community," illustrating a concrete example of someone who has been in similar circumstances and thrived.

Suggestion: When possible, encourage guest speakers to offer internship and volunteer opportunities that can serve to directly connect men of color to career opportunities that may align with their academic interests. As a caution, faculty should remind guest speakers to only offer support and opportunities that can actually be provided. Too often, men of color are made promises that go unfulfilled. It is better to not offer opportunities, than to create false hope.

Critical Reflection

While the prior section examined methods of delivering culturally relevant content, this section is concerned with the interrogation of that content. Critical reflection was another recurrent theme expressed by faculty in the study. As noted by Howard (2003), "critical reflection is the type of processing that is crucial to the concept of culturally relevant pedagogy...[as] reflective action can be a more useful tool for addressing social and emotional issues, namely those issues pertaining to race and culture" (p. 197). Critical reflection involves deep introspection on one's core values, assumptions, actions as well as that of others. Specifically, faculty should provide learning opportunities that encourage students to engage in critical introspection about what they believe, why they believe it, how they interact with others, and how others interpret them. They should be aided in understanding their own ethnic-male cultural worldview.

Moreover, students should also be provided with opportunities to apply the same critical lens to wider society, deconstructing social expectations and values, economic conditions, and structures that systematically disadvantage them. Once understood, they should be empowered to envision ways in which to gain justice in their personal lives, communities, and wider society. Within this context of critical reflection, men of color should be encouraged to consider the goals they have for themselves, why they have chosen these goals, and if such goals will help them change their lives and communities in ways they desire. When employing critical introspection as a component of classroom teaching, faculty members can consider the following topical areas for reflection:

- *Major and Field of Study* – Many students enter community college with multiple goals (e.g., certification, certificate, transfer, associate's degree). However, they should be encouraged to consider if the majors they have declared are real interests or a byproduct of male socialization.
- *Career and Professional Goals* – Students should be encouraged to identify career and professional goals and clearly articulate why they desire to achieve those goals. Students may provide answers that *sound* good (e.g., doctor, lawyer, architect, dentist), but not possess real ambition for those fields. So, reflection must go beyond the surface level.
- *Critical Introspection of Stereotypes* – Students should be presented with information (i.e., statistics from the Department of Justice or Department of Education) that counters specific stereotypes about them (e.g., men of color are criminals, men of color are unintelligent). Then, students should be encouraged to reflect on why data on social statistics may differ so greatly from popular conceptions about men of color.
- *Critical Analysis of Popular Media* – Students should be provided opportunities to deconstruct texts and social scripts portrayed in popular media. Song lyrics, music videos, youtube videos, news stories are a few among many forms of popular media that are ripe for critical analysis. Students should be encouraged to understand the popular assumptions and meanings embodied within these scripts.

Critical reflection is most useful when the topical areas being examined relate directly to the real life experiences of men of color. There are many ways to effectively facilitate critical introspection in course contexts, such as essays, concept mapping, service-learning experiences, and self-assessment inventories (e.g., StrengthsQuest, Myers-Briggs). Chief among these strategies is ongoing reflective journaling. Journaling is a process by which students describe their feelings, dispositions, and thinking about themselves, others, and the world. Journaling can occur in many forms but typically is directed via guided prompts or open-ended expressions of thought. Effective journaling is structured in a manner by which authentic reflection is perceived as beneficial. This is integral, as journaling can be perceived as 'busy-work' when poorly structured.

Critical introspection can be central to men of color's success. Specifically, it can serve as an opportunity for men to voice their opinions and perspectives in ways that they feel comfortable doing. More importantly, introspection can make them aware of how their perceptions and assumptions about themselves, other men of color, and the world are a byproduct of their socialization. Becoming cognizant of the socialization process can enable men to have a greater sense of agency in determining their own goals, ideas, and values separate from those placed on them by wider society. Given the pervasive socialization of boys and young men of color to believe that their success is limited to sports, entertainment, and criminal activity, critical reflection can empower men of color to articulate their *own* goals for their *own* lives.

Collaborative Learning

While lecturing is necessary to convey critical course content, interactivity was a recurrent theme among faculty leaders. While 'stand and deliver' or 'chalk and talk' techniques are widely employed in community colleges, the importance of facilitated engagement and meaningful interaction is essential to men of color's success. Specifically, faculty leaders believed that there was a need to provide students with opportunities to discuss course content via collaborative learning strategies (e.g., working on projects in class with other students, discussing ideas from class with other students, engaging in out-of-class assignments while working with other students). Collaborative learning allows for students to share their personal perspectives while also seeing that there are other students who may share similar challenges. Collaborative learning involves recognition that the faculty member is not the only purveyor of knowledge. This perspective is rooted firmly in Freire's (1970/2005) critique of the banking education model where knowledge is presumed to be 'banked' (or deposited) from teacher to student. In contrast, a more 'dialogic' approach allows for knowledge to emerge from an exchange between teacher-and-student and student-to-student. This learning approach is critical as it can reinforce to men of color that their voices are important in the learning process. This is essential as some men of color are socialized throughout their educational experiences to perceive their voices as being unimportant to classroom discourse. Collaborative learning can also reduce feelings of isolation, helping to alleviate feelings of alienation and to develop a sense of mattering and belonging. In creating a collaborative learning environment, faculty members should:

Restructure Classroom Seating to Facilitate
Collaborative Engagement

Faculty should consider, when appropriate, to restructure the format of classroom seating to adhere to a circular style (for smaller classes) or horseshoe style (for larger classes). While restructuring seating cannot occur for all classes, the benefits are manifold in contexts where it can. In stadium style courses, faculty can consider employing smaller breakout sessions into different rooms or different parts of the same room. Then, faculty can rotate across breakout sessions to check in on students' discussions. Restructuring seating positively disrupts the traditional 'status-quo' arrangement of classroom discourse. This approach 'physically' conveys faculty members' respect for students perspectives and viewpoints; repositioning students as holders of valid knowledge. It can also make disengagement more difficult for students, given that the focus of attention is on one another and not solely on the faculty member.

Provide Opportunities for Students to Work on
Assignments in Small Groups

Small group assignments can be an effective tool for both in-class and out-of-class learning. Faculty can provide opportunities for students to work on discussion based assignments in small clusters (teams of 3-5). To ensure academic rigor, faculty can structure contributions from each team member via effective collaboration rubrics that require students to assess each team member's contribution to the group (see http://edweb.sdsu.edu/triton/tidepoolunit/Rubrics/collrubric. html). Small group assignments foster greater levels of

64

involvement amongst students by allowing them to share multiple perspectives and knowledge. In general education courses, consider grouping students by major. This will allow for students to identify other students in their field who they may encounter in future classes. This approach can support the building of social networks that can be useful in identifying needed resources, collaborating on future assignments, selecting appropriate courses, and determining quality professors. Another approach, is to encourage students to work with other individuals who differ from them in some way (e.g., ethnically, by gender, religion, political affiliation, social class). Engagement with individuals from diverse backgrounds is critical to success for men of color, who are more likely to experience an enhanced sense of belonging when they engage with diverse students.

Suggestion: A critical precursor to collaborative learning is mutual respect among faculty and students. Faculty members must model the expectations and norms for collaboration that they desire to see from students. This includes communicating care and compassion for students and authentic respect for multiple viewpoints that may differ from their own. Students must also be held to high expectations for creating an affirming learning environment for other students as well. This is especially important given that men of color may be apprehensive about engaging in ways that could reify erroneous stereotypes about them and their abilities.

Provide Collaborative Experiential Learning
Opportunities

Experiential learning is a teaching approach that provides opportunities for students to learn through direct experience. Learning by experience can, "include cooperative education placements, practicum experiences, and classroom-based hands-on laboratory activities" (Cantor, 1997, p. 3). Experiential learning can be particularly beneficial for non-traditional learners by providing them with unique opportunities to connect classroom content to real-life experiences. A core component of effective experiential learning is reflection. Students participate in hands-on experiences by engaging in activities that connect to classroom learning. Yet, reflection is what allows students to process the experience, interrogate what was learned, and decipher how that learning complements the theories, concepts, and models discussed in class. In optimal form, students would be clustered into groups to engage in experiential learning opportunities (in and out of class), be provided with opportunities to reflect on their learning, and have opportunities to share their experiences and reflections so that other students can also learn from their learning. Experiential learning is beneficial for all students, but particularly for men of color. Collaborative experiential learning[2] can expose students to different cultural perspectives and experiences, increase their authentic interest in academic content

---

[2] Experiential learning can occur outside of a small group context (i.e., individually); however, the faculty respondents all discussed this concept in context of group or dyadic learning.

(intrinsic interest), and enable them to recognize connections between classroom content and issues related to themselves and their communities. When employing collaborative experiential learning opportunities, faculty members can consider the following learning venues:

- *Library* – Students can engage in historical (archival) research at the campus or local library.
- *Industry* – Students can visit business and industry worksites to develop their professional identities and explore common challenges facing micro, mid-size, and macro-businesses.
- *Community Service* – Students can engage in community service with non-profit organizations and foundations to learn about emerging trends and challenges in their local communities.
- *Campus-Based Service* – Students can participate in campus-based service opportunities, which allow them to engage common student issues and concerns.
- *Investigative Research* – Students can engage in research clusters to investigate research topics of interest to them and relevant to their daily lives.
- *Music or Entertainment Events* – Students can attend cultural music and entertainment events to learn more about different cultures, perspectives, and music genres.
- *Panel/Symposia Presentations* – Students can participate (or attend) panel presentations on current issues in education, technology, politics, and healthcare.
- *Externship Clusters* – Students can engage in short-term externships (1-3 day experiences) to learn about potential professions relevant to their majors.

- *Cultural Immersion Activities* – Students can attend local community-based events that are culturally oriented to learn about communities that differ from their own.

Collaborative experiential learning may be particularly beneficial for men of color, especially when learning opportunity sites are carefully selected by faculty to ensure racial/ethnic and gender diversity among those supporting the experiential learning opportunity. Moreover, collaborative experiential learning can advance their cultural and social capital, by exposing them to opportunities and people that may not be available for them except through course projects.

Performance Monitoring

Monitoring student progress is essential to the success of men of color. Faculty leaders in the study expressed that performance monitoring was a core component of effective teaching for all students, including men of color. According to Wood and Turner (2011), performance monitoring entails, "asking students if they [have] any questions or concerns about the course material as well as reminding them about upcoming deadlines for papers, tests, course reviews, group work, and other assignments" (p. 144). They also noted that performance monitoring involves monitoring students' attendance and assignment outcomes to proactively address concerns before they become larger issues. Based on their perspective, performance monitoring encompasses three core components: (1) asking about questions or concerns, (2) reminding students about timelines, and (3) proactively monitoring assignment outcomes. Altogether, performance monitoring is viewed as being key to establishing an environment where students feel comfortable asking questions about their progress in class.

Monitoring student performance requires faculty members to be organized and up-to-date on grading. It also requires attentiveness to verbal and non-verbal cues, which may infer that a student is unsure about course content. While students should be expected to seek out help when such concerns arise (e.g., a poor grade, missing class, difficulty completing an assignment), it is also important to recall that men of color (like other men) may be apprehensive to seek out help for fear of being perceived as academically inferior. For example, Wood (2014) conducted interviews with 28 African American males attending a community college in the southwestern United States. He found that these men were 'apprehensive to engage' in the classroom for fear of being perceived by faculty and peers as 'stupid,' 'ignorant,' and 'dumb.' He found that this fear of engagement occurred even when students knew the answers to questions asked in class, had questions they needed answered, or desired to go to office hours but felt uncomfortable doing so. He highlighted successful faculty as those who could recognize concerns early on and find ways to approach students one-on-one to encourage and provide them with support. Given the potentially deleterious effect of engagement apprehension on men of color's success, faculty should monitor students' progress and intervene. Moreover, faculty can inculcate and environment of personal success by making attendance at office hours, participation in tutoring, and visiting the library mandatory.

Proactively Asking Students if They Need Help

When proactively monitoring student performance, faculty should provide students opportunities to ask questions in multiple formats (e.g., large group, small group, individually). If it becomes clear that a student may be struggling with the course material, faculty can inquire with the student (one-on-one) about whether they need support. Students should be attuned to whether or not they need support if faculty are providing regular and consistent feedback on assignments and course performance. In some cases, faculty should provide unsolicited help, or ask a student to come to their office hours in order to address minor course challenges early on. One aspect of proactively monitoring student success is making sure that timelines and deadlines are clearly communicated. Faculty should regularly communicate impending deadlines and expectations to all students. Given the intense external pressures faced by non-traditional students, doing so can create a sense of certainty that may not be present in other areas of their academic, personal, and professionals lives. As noted in the previous chapter, caring relationships are critical to teaching men of color. Thus, proactively asking about questions or concerns will only be effective when relationships typified by authenticity, trust, and mutual respect are in place.

Provide Encouragement to Students on the
Margins

Faculty should consider implementing the practice of publically praising students' abilities, successes, talents, and correct answers, especially when their performance is in flux.

Doing so can inspire students to work harder, overcome obstacles, and feel more comfortable seeking help (if needed). While the importance of relationships and positive messaging were addressed extensively in the previous chapter, such relationships and messaging become even more critical when student performance is trending downward. Validating messages that communicate that students belong, can succeed, and have the ability to do college work are critical. Moreover, public encouragement is also essential, but faculty should also communicate authentic realities about their progress. Thus, public praise should be rooted in actual performance, otherwise it may be seen as demeaning or insincere. When necessary, faculty should talk with students one-on-one or after class to let them know that they can do better and to offer additional support and resources. However, such messaging must be conveyed in a manner that demonstrates faculty members' authentic belief in students' academic abilities; otherwise such encounters may serve to detract from, rather than inspire success.

Know When to 'Step In'

Effectively monitoring student performance entails knowing when to 'step in' and intervene. As noted, some men of color may be apprehensive to seek help. Thus, faculty should time interventions to occur early enough in the academic term to allow for successful continuation in the course. Early alert systems can be an effective tool for structuring the timeframe for when an intervention should occur. Early alert systems monitor student success to identify troubling performance indicators (e.g., low scores on exams and major course assignments, excessive absences, missing assignments, incomplete assignments, habitually leaving class early or arriving late). Many course management software, such as Blackboard and Moodle, have early alert systems built in that send messages to faculty when a student's performance meets a critical level. In such cases, faculty members can then refer students to services (e.g., tutoring, financial aid, personal counseling, academic advising, disability services) that can support their continuation and success in class.

In all, the four areas of teaching excellence identified in this chapter (e.g., content relevancy, critical reflection, collaborative learning, and performance monitoring) can serve to improve outcomes for men of color in community college. As noted, these areas are not necessarily unique to men of color, but can have an intensified benefit to their success due to external pressures in their lives, preK-12 experiences of classroom marginalization, and the socialization of men of color in wider society. The next chapter concludes this guidebook by offering recommendations to instructional leaders on how they can better support faculty members to teach men of color effectively.

PART IV

A NOTE TO INSTRUCTIONAL LEADERS

While the preceding chapters articulated strategies for teaching men of color in community college, implementing these approaches may take additional support from instructional leaders (e.g., department chairs, faculty development professionals, academic deans, vice presidents of instruction). As a result, beyond providing recommendations for their peers, faculty leaders also extended suggestions for college leaders. Specifically, these suggestions focused on steps and strategies that instructional leaders could take to improve the success of men of color. Collectively, the recommendations offered address issues of training, policies, messaging, and perspectives held by faculty members about men of color. Faculty members must embrace an internal locus of control, believing that they possess the capacity to advance success for men of color and other disadvantaged student groups. To bolster this perspective, the overwhelming majority of faculty leaders indicated that professional development programming was needed to better prepare faculty members to work with men of color. However, given the historical avoidance of professional development programming geared towards this population, faculty leaders overwhelmingly suggested that programming should be mandatory in nature.

While many topical areas were recommended for professional development, the most recurrent training needs included (in rank order): (a) cultural sensitivity and competency; (b) racial and gender stereotypes; (c) understanding the complex challenges and realities of men of color; and (d) collaborative teaching and learning strategies (see Table 1). Other recommendations featured counselor-based training for faculty, such as development activities in: humanistic psychology, client centered therapy, displaying unconditional positive regard, and building trust with men of color. Lastly, it should be noted that several contributors noted that professional development activities could incorporate the participation of men of color, using professional development programming as an avenue to foster critical, honest dialogues between men of color and faculty members.

Table 1.

Recommendations for Professional Development Programming

Professional Development Recommendations
1. Required Professional Development for Faculty
2. Imbedding Cultural Competence into Retention, Tenure, and Promotion Policies
3. Communicate Faculty Members' Responsibility to Building Students' Confidence
4. Ensure that Faculty Members Communicate High Expectations to Students
5. Revise Hiring Policies to Increase Faculty Diversity and Connectedness with Students
6. Communicate the Importance of Student Success to Faculty Early on and Regularly
7. Institutionalizing Retention Programs with a Proven Track Record

While professional development was the primary recommendation from faculty leaders, other areas of intervention were also suggested. Several faculty leaders recommended that culturally competent requirements for teaching and learning be imbedded into institutional retention, promotion, and tenure processes. These faculty members extolled the importance of holding faculty members accountable for continuous improvement in demonstrating cultural competence in working with diverse student groups. In addition, faculty leaders highlighted the importance of students' confidence. Specifically, they noted that men of color often have more limited confidence in their academic abilities. This could be due to prior racialized messages expressed to them in preK-12 education. Faculty leaders recommended that institutional leaders strongly communicate to faculty that helping build students' confidence is a key responsibility. As part of faculty members' roles in building students' confidence, several faculty leaders suggested that faculty members must have and communicate high expectations for students' ability to succeed and their academic aptitude. They also noted that faculty should hold students accountable to those high standards of performance within their zone of proximal development.

Faculty leaders noted that some of their peers may not be equipped or desire to serve complex student demographic populations. As such, they recommended that hiring policies be revised to increase diversity and ensure that new hires (both White and of color) have the predisposition to educate diverse students. Faculty contributors noted that the importance and concern for student success should be communicated to faculty early on in their tenure at the institution. Moreover, student success should also be a topic addressed on a regular basis. In doing so, conversations on student success can be elevated to prominence within common institutional discourse. Faculty leaders also expressed the importance of supporting existing programs (e.g., retention programs, achievement programs) and initiatives serving historically underrepresented and underserved students, particularly men of color. They noted that initiatives with a proven track record of success in serving men of color should be institutionalized with stable funding streams to ensure programmatic viability. Instructional leaders can support the sustainability of these programs by collaborating with student affairs professionals to advocate for them.

It is also critical that instructional leaders foster a culture of analysis to evaluate whether their respective subunits are prepared to meet the needs of men of color. In 2013, M2C3 created the Community College Student Success Inventory (CCSSI). The CCSSI is a self-assessment inventory designed to be used by leaders in determining readiness to serve men of color in six overarching categories: (1) financial aid, (2) student support services, (3) teaching and learning, (4) institutional research, (5) minority male initiatives and programs, and (6) early alert systems (see Harris & Wood, 2014a). Each overarching area is accompanied with items that campuses can use to determine their areas of strength and those in need of improvement. Relevant to this guidebook are items in the overarching category on teaching and learning (See Table 2).

Table 2

CCSSI Teaching and Learning Subconstruct

		Strongly Disagree	Disagree	Somewhat Disagree	Somewhat Agree	Agree	Strongly Agree
3.1	Faculty-student interaction is assessed in course evaluations.	○	○	○	○	○	○
3.2	Students' perceptions of affirmation from faculty are incorporated into course evaluations.	○	○	○	○	○	○
3.3	Educators are well-versed in issues that influence the success of men of color.	○	○	○	○	○	○
3.4	Faculty members receive on-going training in culturally relevant teaching strategies.	○	○	○	○	○	○
3.5	Relevant student support services are highlighted in course syllabi.	○	○	○	○	○	○
3.6	Relevant student support services are discussed by classroom faculty.	○	○	○	○	○	○
3.7	Prospective faculty hires are assessed for their competency to engage diverse student populations.	○	○	○	○	○	○
3.8	The racial/gender composition of the faculty reflects that of the student body.	○	○	○	○	○	○
3.9	Men of color are equitably represented among students who participate in learning communities (e.g., first year experience, Puente).	○	○	○	○	○	○

Table 2

(continued)

	Strongly Disagree	Disagree	Somewhat Disagree	Somewhat Agree	Agree	Strongly Agree
3.10 Academic policies are in place for students to repeat coursework without being heavily penalized.	○	○	○	○	○	○
3.11 Men of color are equitably represented on the institution's dean's lists.	○	○	○	○	○	○
3.12 Men of color are equitably represented among students who participate in "prestigious" academic programs.	○	○	○	○	○	○
3.13 Men of color are equitably represented among students who graduate with honors.	○	○	○	○	○	○

The CCSSI has thirteen statements relevant to teaching and learning. Example statements include: "Faculty members receive on-going training in culturally relevant teaching strategies," "relevant student support services are highlighted in course syllabi," and "academic policies are in place for students to repeat coursework without being heavily penalized." Instructional leaders can use this section of the CCSSI by assembling faculty members in their respective subunits and working collectively through the statements to generate consensus on responses. Responses to the items may help to identify areas for improvement, reveal hidden assumptions about policies and practices in place, and to provide a 'roadmap' on new approaches for implementation. The CCSSI has been subjected to rigorous tests for content validity, both for the individual items and the total scales (see Harris & Wood, 2014a). Thus, the instrument can be used as an effective tool for determining curricular preventions and interventions.

Instructional leaders are also encouraged to use institutional data to further determine specific sites for intervention. Based on student success data for men of color, instructional leaders can identify courses that serve as gatekeepers to student success. Possibly, professional development programming may be warranted to increase faculty members' capacities to serve men of color. Of course, any such efforts should be encompassed within the broad spectrum of program review, so that interventions are used for continuous improvement rather than to 'target' specific subunits or individuals. Overall, student success for men of color can be improved through a culture of analysis that identifies student needs, monitors progress of students in curricular pathways, and evaluates student outcomes (e.g., personal, learning, career).

REFERENCES

AACC. (2014). Staff employment distribution. Washington, DC: American Association of Community Colleges. Retrieved November 3, 2014 from http://www.aacc.nche.edu/AboutCC/Trends/Pages/staffemploymentdistribution.aspx

Alloway, N. (1995). Foundation stones: The construction of gender in early childhood. Carlton, Vic: Curriculum Corporation.

Anderson, L. W. (1975). Student involvement in learning and school achievement. California Journal of Educational Research, 26, 53-62.

Astin, A. W. (1984). Student involvement: A developmental theory for higher education. Journal of College Student Personnel, 25, 297–308.

Astin, A. W. (1993). What matters in college? Four critical years revisited. San Francisco, CA: Jossey-Bass.

Bensimon, E. M. (2005). Closing the achievement gap in higher education: An organizational learning perspective. New Directions for Higher Education, 131, 99-111.

BPS. (2009). U.S. Department of Education, 2003-2004 Beginning Postsecondary Students Longitudinal Study, Second Fellow-UP (BPS:04/09). Computation by NCES PowerStats on 7/31/2014. Washington, DC: National Center for Education Statistics.

Bush, E. C., & Bush, L. (2010). Calling out the elephant: An examination of African American male achievement in community colleges. Journal of African American Males in Education, 1, 40–62.

Cantor, J. A. (1997). Experiential learning in higher education: Linking classroom and community. Washington, DC: Eric Digest.

Christian, K. (2010). AACC launches minority male student success database. Washington, DC: American Association of Community Colleges. Retrieved May 12, 2011, from http://www.aacc.nche.edu/newsevents/News/articles/Pages/012220101.aspx

de la Garza, T., Wood, J. L., & Harris III, F. (2014). An exploratory assessment of the validity of the Community College Survey of Men (CCSM): Implications for serving veteran men. Community College Journal of Research and Practice, 39(3), 293-298. doi:10.1080/10668926.2014.942758

Essien-Wood, I. (2010). Undergraduate African American females in the sciences: A qualitative study of student experiences affecting academic success and persistence (Unpublished doctoral dissertation). Arizona State University, Tempe, AZ.

Feistritzer, E. C. (2011). Profile of teachers in the U.S.-2011. Washington, DC: National Center for Education Information.

Freire, P. (2005). Pedagogy of the oppressed (30th anniv. Ed). New York, NY: Continuum.

Gardenhire-Crooks, A., Collado, H., Martin, K., & Castro, A. (2010). Terms of engagement: Men of color discuss their experiences in community college. New York, NY: MDRC.

Harper, S. R. (2014). (Re)setting the agenda for college men of color: Lessons learned from a 15-year movement to improve Black male student success. In R. A. Williams (Ed.), Men of color in higher education: New foundations for developing models for success (pp. 116-143). Sterling, VA: Stylus.

Harper, S. R., & Wood, J. L. (Eds.). (2015). Advancing Black male student success from preschool through PhD. Sterling, VA: Stylus.

Harris III, F., Bensimon, E. M., & Bishop, R. (2010). The equity scorecard: A process for building institutional capacity to educate young men of color. In C. Edley, Jr. & J. Ruiz de Velasco (Eds.), Changing places: How communities will improve the health of boys of color (pp. 277-308). Berkeley: University of California Press.

Harris III, F., & Harper, S. R. (2008). Masculinities go to community college: Understanding male identity socialization and gender role conflict. New Directions for Community Colleges, 142, 25-35.

Harris III, F., & Wood, J. L. (2014a). Community College Student Success Inventory (CCSSI) for men of color in community colleges: Content validation summary. Community College Journal of Research and Practice. doi: 10.1080/10668926.2014.880165

Harris III, F., & Wood, J. L. (2014b). Examining the status of men of color in California community colleges: Recommendations for state policymakers. San Diego, CA: Minority Male Community College Collaborative (M2C3).

Howard, T. C. (2003). Culturally relevant pedagogy: Ingredients for critical teacher reflection. Theory into Practice, 42(3), 195-202.

Kuh, G. D. (2009). What student affairs professionals need to know about student engagement. Journal of College Student Development, 50(6), 83–706.

Ladson-Billings, G. (1995). But that's just good teaching! The case for culturally relevant pedagogy. Theory into Practice, 43(3), 159-165.

Ladson-Billings, G. (1992). Liberatory consequences of literacy: A case of culturally relevant instruction for African American students. Journal of Negro Education, 61(3), 378-391.

Mullin, C. M. (2012). Student success: Institutional and individual perspectives. Community College Review, 40(2), 126-144.

Nevarez, C., & Wood, J. L. (2010). Community college leadership and administration: Theory, practice, and change. New York, NY: Peter Lang.

NPSAS. (2012). U.S. Department of Education, 2012. National Postsecondary Student Aid Study (NPSAS: 2012). Computation by NCES Powerstats on 8/2/2014. Washington, DC: National Center for Education Statistics.

O'Neil, J. (1981). Patterns of gender role conflict and strain: Sexism and fear of femininity of men's lives. The Personnel and Guidance Journal, 60(4), 203-210.

Pace, C. R. (1984). Measuring the quality of college student experiences: An account of the development and use of the College Student Experiences Questionnaire. Los Angeles, CA: Higher Education Research Institute.

Rendón, L. I. (1994). Validating culturally diverse students: Toward a new model of learning and student development. Innovative Higher Education, 19(1), 33-50

Sáenz, V. B., Bukoski, B. E., Lui, C., & Rodriguez, S. (2013). Latino males in Texas community colleges: A phenomenological study of masculinity constructs and their effect on college experiences. Journal of African American Males in Education, 4(2), 82-102.

Sanford, N. (1966). Self and society. New York, NY: Atherton.

Steele, C. M. (1997). A threat in the air: How stereotypes shape intellectual identity and performance. American Psychologist, 52, 613–629.

Steele, C. M. (1999). Thin ice: Stereotype threat and Black college students. The Atlantic Online. Retrieved from http://www.theatlantic.com/magazine/archive/1999/08/thin-ice-stereotype-threat-and-black-college-students/304663/6/

Strayhorn, T. L. (2012). College students' sense of belonging: A key to educational success for all students. New York, NY: Routledge.

Sue, D. W., Capodilupo, C. M., Torino, G. C., Bucceri, J. M., Holder, A. M. B., Nadal, K. L., & Esquilin, M. E. (2007). Racial microaggressions in everyday life: Implications for clinical practice. American Psychologist, 62(4), 271-286.

The Seven Centers Report. (2014). Advancing the success of boys and men of color: Recommendations for policy makers. Contributions from the Center for the Study of Race and Equity in Education, Minority Male Community College Collaborative, Morehouse Research Institute, Project MALES and the Texas Education Consortium for Male Students of Color, Todd Anthony Bell National Resource Center on the African American Male, Black Male Institute, Wisconsin's Equity and Inclusion Laboratory. San Diego, CA: Printing Office.

Tinto, V. (1987). Leaving college: Rethinking the causes and cures of student attrition (2nd ed.). Chicago, IL: The University of Chicago Press

White House. (2014). My brother's keeper. Retrieved November 2, 2014, from http://www.whitehouse.gov/my-brothers-keeper

Wood, J. L. (2010). African American males in the community college: Towards a model of academic success (Unpublished doctoral dissertation). Arizona State University, Tempe, AZ.

Wood, J. L. (2014). Apprehension to engagement in the classroom: Perceptions of Black males in the community college. International Journal of Qualitative Studies in Education, 27(6), 785-803.

Wood, J. L., & Essien-Wood, I. (2012). Capital identity projection: Understanding the psychosocial effects of capitalism on Black male community college students. Journal of Economic Psychology, 33, 984-995.

Wood, J. L., & Harris III, F. (2013). The Community College Survey of Men: An initial validation of the instrument's non-cognitive outcomes construct. Community College Journal of Research and Practice, 37, 333-338.

Wood, J. L., Harris III, F., & Xiong, S. (2014). Advancing the success of men of color in the community college: Special issue on the Community College Survey of Men. Journal of Progressive Policy & Practice, 2(2), 129-133.

Wood, J. L., & Harrison, J. D. (2014). The 2020 American Graduation Initiative: A clear vision or dim view. In E. M. Zamani-Gallaher (Ed.), The Obama administration and educational reform (pp. 119-139). Bingley, UK: Emerald.

Wood, J. L., & Palmer, R. T. (2014). Black male students in higher education: A guide to ensuring success. New York, NY: Routledge.

Wood, J. L., & Turner, C. S. V. (2011). Black males and the community college: Student perspectives on faculty and academic success. Community College Journal of Research and Practice, 35, 135-151.

Wood, J. L. & Williams, R. (2013). Persistence factors for Black males in the community college: An examination of background, academic, social, and environmental variables. Spectrum: A Journal on Black Men, 1(2), 1-28.

ABOUT THE AUTHORS

J. Luke Wood, PhD, is Associate Professor of Community College Leadership and the Director of the Doctoral Program Concentration in Community College Leadership at San Diego State University (SDSU). Dr. Wood is also Co-Director of the Minority Male Community College Collaborative (M2C3), Chair-Elect for the Council on Ethnic Participation (CEP) for the Association for the Study of Higher Education (ASHE), and Director of the Center for African American Research and Policy (CAARP). He is also the Co-Editor of the Journal of Applied Research in the Community College (JARCC). Wood's research focuses on factors affecting the success of men of color in the community college. In particular, his research examines contributors to student persistence, achievement, attainment, and transfer for these men. Dr. Wood has authored over 80 publications, including five co-authored books, five edited books, and 40 peer-reviewed journal articles.

Frank Harris III, EdD, is an Associate Professor of postsecondary education and Co-Director of the Minority Male Community College Collaborative (M2C3) at San Diego State University. His research is broadly focused on student development and student success in postsecondary education and explores questions related to the social construction of gender and race on college campuses, college men and masculinities, and racial/ethnic disparities in college student outcomes. Before joining the faculty at San Diego State, Harris worked as a student affairs educator and college administrator in the areas of student affairs administration, student crisis support and advocacy, new student orientation programs, multicultural student affairs, academic advising, and enrollment services. His most recent administrative appointment was at the University of Southern California as Associate Director of the Center for Urban Education. Harris earned his Ed.D. in Higher Education from the University of Southern California Rossier School of Education.

Khalid White, EdD, is an Ethnic Studies Professor and Umoja Program Coordinator at San Jose City College. Khalid began teaching in the California Community College system in 2005, in the Ethnic Studies and Social Science disciplines. Prior to working in higher education, Khalid worked with incarcerated adolescents in the Juvenile Probation field. His research and practical efforts in higher education have focused on effective strategies for student success for African American males, and underrepresented males, in the California Community College system. Dr. White received his Bachelor's degree in Sociology from Morehouse College. He earned a Master's degree in Adolescent Education from Harvard University's Graduate School of Education. Khalid completed his Doctorate degree in Education Leadership at the University of California Davis and Sonoma State University.

CPSIA information can be obtained
at www.ICGtesting.com
Printed in the USA
LVHW071959270621
691281LV00020B/2978